P9-DHS-279

CHRIST
in the Passover

CEIL &
MOISHE ROSEN

CHRIST
in the Passover

MOODY PUBLISHERS
CHICAGO

© 2006 by
CEIL & MOISHE ROSEN

All rights reserved. No part of this book may be reproduced in any form without permission in writing from the publisher, except in the case of brief quotations embodied in critical articles or reviews.

All Scripture quotations, unless otherwise indicated, are taken from the *Holy Bible, New International Version*®. NIV®. Copyright © 1973, 1978, 1984 by International Bible Society. Used by permission of Zondervan Publishing House. All rights reserved.

Scripture quotations marked KJV are taken from the King James Version.

Quotations from Maccabees are taken from Bruce M. Metzger, ed. *The Oxford Annotated Apocrypha* (New York: Oxford University Press, 1977).

All italics added to Scripture are the author's emphasis.

Cover Design: DesignWorks Group Inc.
Cover Image: www.thedesignworksgroup.com
Cover Photography by: Steve Gardner, PixelWorks Studios, www.ShootPW.com http://www.ShootPW.com
Editor: Ali Diaz

Library of Congress Cataloging-in-Publication Data

Rosen, Ceil.
   Christ in the Passover / Ceil and Moishe Rosen.
      p. cm.
   Includes bibliographical references and index.
   ISBN-13: 978-0-8024-1389-5
   1. Jesus Christ—Passion. 2. Passover. I. Rosen, Moishe. II. Title.

BT431.3.R67 2006
263'.97—dc22

2006005977

ISBN-10: 0-8024-1389-7
ISBN-13: 978-0-8024-1389-5

We hope you enjoy this book from Moody Publishers.
Our goal is to provide high quality, thought-provoking books and products that connect truth to your real needs and challenges.
For more information on other books and products written and produced from a biblical perspective, go to www.moodypublishers.com or write to:

Moody Publishers
820 N. LaSalle Boulevard
Chicago, IL 60610

1 3 5 7 9 10 8 6 4 2

Printed in the United States of America

CONTENTS

GLOSSARY

Aphikomen (*afikomen*). Hebrew translations for Greek derivative, *epikomios*. That which comes last, the hidden Passover bread eaten at the seder.

Ashkenazim. Hebrew for a cultural branch of Judaism that developed in northern and eastern Europe and from which most American Jews are descended.

Bedikat Chametz. Hebrew for the formal search for leaven before Passover.

Betzah. Hebrew for "egg," symbolic hardboiled and roasted egg on the seder plate; also called *Haggigah*.

Booths, Feast of. In Hebrew, *Succoth*, the fifteenth day of the seventh month of the Jewish calendar; a seven-day holiday when Israel was to dwell in booths in commemoration of the wilderness wanderings.

Chametz (*chometz*). Hebrew for any fermented product of grain and all leavening agents; that which makes sour.

Charoseth. Hebrew for a mixture of apples, cinnamon, and nuts representing the mortar of Egypt; one of the symbolic foods on the seder plate.

Chazereth. Hebrew for a whole piece of, or a whole, bitter root, usually horseradish, on the seder plate.

Dayenu. Hebrew title of a Passover song meaning, "it would have been sufficient."

Echad. Hebrew for "one."

Feasts of Jehovah. The seven holidays that God commanded Israel to observe on the second day of the Feast of Unleavened Bread.

Galatianism. A heresy that insisted that in order to be truly Christian, non-Jews must be circumcised and obey the Law.

Gamaliel. A celebrated rabbi of the early part of the first century; the teacher of the apostle Paul.

Gentile. Of or pertaining to any people who are not Jewish.

Haggadah. Hebrew for the book that sets forth and explains the seder service.

Haggigah. Hebrew for the festival offering; the other sacrifice offered in the Temple in addition to the Paschal lamb.

Hallel. Hebrew for "praise, a prayer of praise"; Psalms 113 to 118. The Great Hallel is Psalm 136.

Hillel. A famous rabbi of the time of Herod, thought to be Gamaliel's grandfather.

Judaize. To bring non-Jews to accept the obligations of rabbinical tradition. See *Galatianism*.

Karpas. Hebrew for one of the symbolic foods on the seder plate, usually parsley or other greens.

Kiddush. Hebrew for a prayer of sanctification; the blessing over the ritual cup of wine.

Kiporah. Hebrew for "covering"; atonement that covers sin.

Kitel. A long, white robe worn by Orthodox Jews at certain holidays and as a burial garment.

Levites. The tribe of Levi; the hereditary lineage from which came the priests and others who ministered in the Temple.

Maror. Hebrew for bitter, ground horseradish, one of the symbolic foods on the seder plate.

Matzo. Hebrew for "without leaven"; a flat wafer of unleavened bread.

Matzo Tash. Yiddish for a baglike fabric container used for the three ritual wafers of unleavened bread at the seder.

Messiah. English translation of Hebrew *mashiach*, meaning "the anointed One of God" who was to come to fill all three offices for which one must receive anointing: prophet, priest, and king; the promised Redeemer.

Mishnah. Hebrew for the collection of oral law that forms the basis of the Talmud; compiled by Judah ha-Nasi (c. AD 135 to 220).

Mount Sinai. The mountain from which God gave the Law to Moses.

Nisan. The first month in the Jewish calendar, also known as *Abib*.

Pascha. Greek translation of the Hebrew *pesah*, meaning "Passover."

Passover. From the Hebrew *pesah*; the first of the seven feasts of Jehovah; the Paschal sacrifice; title may also include Feast of Unleavened Bread.

Pentecost. The Feast of Weeks (*Shavuot*); the fiftieth day after the first day of the Feast of Unleavened Bread; the festival of the gathering of the first fruits of the wheat harvest.

Pesah. Hebrew for the holiday of Passover; the Paschal lamb.

Pesahim. Hebrew. A section of Talmudic commentary on the feast of the Passover.

Pharisees. A strict religious party who were known for their zealous adherence to the teaching of the rabbis concerning the Law. Their chief doctrine was that salvation and God's favor would come as a result of keeping the Law.

Priests. Descendants of Aaron (of the tribe of Levi) who officiated at religious services in the Temple; they also served as judges, physicians, and teachers.

Sadducees. An ancient sect of Judaism whose views and practices were opposed to those of the Pharisees. They denied the authority of oral tradition, the resurrection of the dead, and the existence of angels.

Sanhedrin. The legislative and judicial parliament supposedly descendant from the Babylonian captivity.

Seder. Hebrew for "set order"; the ritual Passover meal that is observed in specific order.

Sephardim. Hebrew for a cultural branch of Judaism; descendants of the Jews who fled Spain and Portugal after the Edict of Expulsion in 1492. They share a common language known as *Ladino* (a variant of Spanish), as opposed to northern European (Ashkenazi) Jews, who speak Yiddish (a Germanic dialect).

Shemah. Hebrew for the most widely known Jewish confession of faith in one God; the first word of Deuteronomy 6:4, from which the prayer derives its name.

Siddur. Hebrew for the Jewish prayer book; the set order of prayers.

Talmud. The two commentaries on the Mishnah, one produced in the Holy Land about AD 275, the other in Babylonia about AD 500; the designation for both the Mishnah and the commentaries on it (*Gemara*).

Torah. Hebrew for the Pentateuch; the first five books of the Bible; the Law given to Moses; the scroll containing the first five books of the Bible, used in the synagogue.

Unleavened Bread, Feast of. The second of the seven feasts of Jehovah, which begins on the fifteenth of Nisan. Directly after the Passover, it continues for seven days. It is sometimes included in the festival of Passover, whereby the two are designated as one holiday lasting eight days. No leaven is to be eaten.

Ur. An ancient Sumerian city and district in southern Babylonia by the Euphrates River; the home of Abraham.

Yarmulke. A cap worn by Orthodox Jews during prayers.

Yiddish. The language spoken by Jews of European ancestry; it is a dialect of old German.

Zeroah. Hebrew for "arm"; in animals, "shoulder"; the shank bone on the seder plate representative of the Paschal sacrifice (occasionally a chicken neck if a lamb shank is unobtainable).

Jehovah chose Israel . . .

INTRODUCTION
He who has an ear, let him hear.
(Revelation 13:9)

The Jews are God's chosen people. This is the inescapable teaching of Scripture. Yet that small statement is enough to disquiet many. No one is more confused by the election of Israel than the Jewish people themselves. To be chosen is a high honor, but how do a people live up to it? Some have wondered: "Why us? If being chosen by God means undergoing the persecution and suffering our people have experienced, maybe it would have been better for us if He had chosen someone else!" Nevertheless, God *did* choose *Israel*. He did not choose her as a pet people to be pampered, nor did He single her out for persecutions and distress.

Jehovah chose Israel *to teach all nations of Himself*—to be a witness of the existence of the one true God:

"You are my witnesses," declares the LORD, "and my servant whom I have chosen . . . I, am the LORD . . . You are my witnesses," declares the LORD, "that I am God." (Isaiah 43:10–12)

Jehovah chose Israel *to show His love and faithfulness:*

The LORD did not set his affection on you and choose you because you were more numerous . . . for you were the fewest of all peoples. But it was because the LORD loved you and kept the oath he swore to your forefathers. (Deuteronomy 7:7–8)

Jehovah chose Israel *to be a blessing to all people* through the seed of Abraham:

The LORD had said to Abram, . . . "I will make you into a great nation and I will bless you; . . . and you will be a blessing . . . and all peoples on earth will be blessed through you." (Genesis 12:1–3)

Jehovah chose Israel *to be a praise to Him:*

This people have I formed for myself; they shall shew forth my praise. (Isaiah 43:21 KJV)

Jehovah chose Israel *to bring salvation to all people:*

You Samaritans worship what you do not know; we worship what we do know, for salvation is from the Jews. (John 4:22)

Through Israel came the holy writings, the promises of God, and the Redeemer. Sometimes the people of Israel were unwilling vessels. But God used even their lapses of faith and disobedience as lessons for those who wanted to know Him. The chosen people will serve God in one way or another, but the joy of serving Him comes only from a relationship with Him.

All that happened to ancient Israel has a direct bearing on God's people today. The apostle Paul wrote in 1 Corinthians 10:11, "These things happened to them [Israel] as examples and were written down as warnings for us, on whom the fulfillment of the ages has come."

Everything the people of Israel did, both as a nation and as individuals, can be a lesson to us today. Through the history of Israel, we see the hand of the Almighty guiding, directing, and showing what He expects of His people. Israel's customs are more than quaint folklore studied by historians and anthropologists. Her history is a memorial of the past and a guidepost to the future.

In the saga of His special people, Israel, God shows humanity:

1. The unsatisfactory condition of the natural human heart,
2. His willingness to forgive and restore,
3. The way He has provided that all people might come to Him, and
4. The faithfulness and constancy of His love.

From the loins of Abraham, God formed this people. He called Abraham out of paganism and idolatry and established his seed to be a great nation to be an example to the Gentiles. He gave His people a Law and a land. He commanded them to keep the Sabbath as a reminder of creation and their Creator, and He ordained seven religious feasts to be observed every year (Leviticus 23:5–44). First, Israel had to learn from her own history to come to trust the one true God. His dealings with the Jewish people became a beacon to steer all the nations away from idolatry and sin to saving faith in their Creator.

The events and teachings in Scripture often have more than one meaning. Contemporary events can have one or more prophetic counterparts. There can also be spiritual applications. The ancient feasts of Jehovah cast the shadow of a greater future reality. There was a threefold significance to those annual festivals: first, they were seasonal celebrations based on the agrarian culture of that time; second, they reminded Israel of God's dealings with them; and third, they pointed to a future promise.

As God ordered the universe and commanded the seasons of nature, He ordained times and seasons to usher in His plan of salvation for the human race. Israel's feasts of Jehovah portray stages of God's dealings with humanity, which culminate in the completion of the plan of salvation.

*They knew they needed to be delivered,
not only from Pharaoh but also from Egypt . . .*

Chapter One

WHY PASSOVER?

When Abraham, the first Hebrew, left Ur to follow God's call, he sacrificed a life of comfort and ease. Ur was no small village. It was one of the oldest, most important cities of Mesopotamia, covering an area of about four square miles by the Euphrates River, which empties into the Persian Gulf. The citizens of Ur, numbering well over half a million, lived in walled safety. They enjoyed the advantages of the highest culture and civilization of their time. The outstanding architecture of their temples, which they built in honor of their numerous deities, was a source of great pride.

From the comfort, advantages, and sophistication of Ur, Jehovah called Abraham and his family to a seminomadic way of life. They were not nomads in spirit, for they were headed for the Promised Land, but they did not yet possess it. They wandered with the seasons, seeking pasture for their flocks, and they also tilled the ground. Tents were their only shelter from the scorching sun and cruel desert wind. But they believed that one day the land really would be theirs, evidenced by their burying those who died along the way in permanent caves.

Then a great drought and famine drove Jacob, a grandson of Abraham, to leave Canaan for the promise of food in Egypt. Once again the seed of Abraham dismantled their tents. Packing all that they had left, they headed south with their wives, their little ones, and their flocks. Because Jacob's son Joseph had found favor with the current pharaoh, they were welcomed as honored quests and given the land of Goshen as their dwelling place (Genesis 47:6). Goshen was a fertile area along the delta of the Nile River, lying in the northeast portion of an area between what is now Cairo to the southeast and Alexandria to the northwest. Here the Hebrews felt respected and secure.

EGYPT IS OUR HOME— WHY BOTHER ABOUT CANAAN?

B ecause of the devastating drought that drove Jacob to seek refuge in Egypt, many of the Egyptians eventually ran out of food too. Some sold their cattle, their land, and finally themselves to Pharaoh in exchange for room and board. Because the pharaohs of that time were of Semitic descent, they favored the seed of Abraham, who also were Semites. For the first time since Abraham left Ur, the Hebrews enjoyed a feeling or permanence. They lived a quiet, secure life in Goshen. The Nile overflowed its banks once a year, bringing life-giving water to the earth. There was lush, abundant pasture for the flocks and rich soil to grow their food.

Here the Hebrews watched their children grow tall and brown in the sun. At night they slept in safety behind the thick walls of their adobe homes. No longer did they wake to the distressed bleating of hungry flocks. Their Egyptian neighbors were people of high morals and advanced culture. Not only did they produce literature and music, but they also knew mathematics and some of the healing arts, and many were skilled architects. They accepted the Hebrews as equals and even bestowed high honors on some of them. Life was pleasant indeed.

Under these circumstances the descendants of Abraham prospered for hundreds of years. Exodus 1:9 indicates they multiplied so fast that a later pharaoh grew concerned that there were more Hebrews than Egyptians in the land. The children of Israel were so comfortable and secure that it was easy to forget that Egypt was not the land God had promised to their fathers. Maybe some of them even forgot God Himself.

They were no longer following God's directives. The covenant Jehovah had made with Abraham was two-sided. On God's part, He promised them land (Genesis 15:18). On Abraham's part, he and his seed were to go where they were told and bear the physical marks of the covenant-circumcision (Genesis 17:10). The Hebrews forgot to seek the Promised Land and forgot to circumcise while they were in Egypt (Joshua 5:5). They would need to be redeemed, to be "deemed again" the people of the covenant, the people of God.

O LORD, FORGIVE OUR COMPLACENCY— GET US OUT OF HERE!

For more than four hundred years the Israelites lived at the edge of a volcano without knowing it. The volcano that was Egypt erupted and its flames threatened to consume them, for there arose a new pharaoh who "did not know about Joseph" (Exodus 1:8). Fearing the strength and power of the vast multitude of Hebrew foreigners, he turned against them and made them his slaves. The children of Israel continued to live in Goshen, but the land no longer belonged to them. Now they belonged to the land, to Egypt, and to the pharaoh. They had to serve him with backbreaking labor, sweating in the fields, building his treasured cities, without compensation or even dignity. There were no strikes or unions to file a complaint. Pharaoh appointed foremen to give his slaves more work than they could do. If a man dropped from exhaustion, the taskmasters left him to die and quickly whipped another into line to take his place.

Under this regime, the children of Israel toiled and suffered, but still they grew in number. Enraged, Pharaoh ordered the Hebrews' male babies murdered in an attempt to wipe out the entire nation. Then the Israelites remembered the God of their fathers. They knew they needed to be delivered, not only from Pharaoh but also from Egypt. They cried out to God in their bondage and distress, and He heard their anguished pleas. Now that they were ready for His help, He remembered His covenant with Abraham, with Isaac, and with Jacob. Deliverance was near.

Jehovah could have slain the wicked pharaoh in an instant and brought about a new, more favorable order in Egypt. But that would not have been enough. The sons of Jacob had to leave Egypt in order to serve God. Old things, old attitudes, old affections had to pass away. The nation of Israel also needed a new beginning. Thus the redemption at Passover prepared the sons of Jacob for another covenant to be made at Mount Sinai, which would reestablish and reaffirm them as the nation of God.

The Passover redemption from Egypt changed Israel's

reckoning of time.[1] God commanded the Hebrews to count the month of the deliverance from Egypt as the first month of the year. He was basically saying, "This event is so historic that you are to rearrange your calendar because of it." They were to start counting their history from the month of *Nisan*. (Similarly, we mark our history BC and AD, basing our calendar on what happened at Calvary.) The great nation that God had promised to Abraham was about to become a reality.

Israel's redemption began that night behind the safety of blood-sprinkled doors . . .

Chapter Two

THE ORIGINAL PASSOVER

In order to redeem His people from Egypt, Jehovah chose a man who was, in many ways, as much an Egyptian as he was a Hebrew. Moses was born an Israelite, but he grew to manhood in the palace of Pharaoh's daughter. He was raised by his Hebrew mother, but he learned worldly wisdom from Egyptian schoolmasters. God chose him to deliver Israel, to show to all that "the Lord makes a distinction between Egypt and Israel" (Exodus 11:7).

As a young man, Moses fled Egypt in disgrace under penalty of death. When God called him to lead Israel out of bondage, he had been away from Egypt's culture and sophistication for forty years. He had long given up his princely robes for the rough garb of a shepherd. He would stand before the successor to the pharaoh who had sought his life. His eyes blazed with the fire of the living God, whom he had encountered in the wilderness. His hands, calloused by the shepherd's crook, wielded a staff that was an instrument of God's power. His lips were the mouthpiece of the Lord as he confronted Pharaoh with his words: "Let my people go!"

When Pharaoh refused, the Lord demonstrated His might by bringing down judgment on Egypt's false gods. Through Moses, He turned the water into blood, showing He was greater than the Nile, which the Egyptians worshiped as the sustainer of life. He darkened the sky, proclaiming His superiority over the sun god, Ra. He made pests of the frogs, which Egyptians had respected as controllers of the undesirable insects that followed the annual overflow of the great river.

While the Lord poured out plague after plague, Pharaoh's heart was still hard. God ruined the Egyptians' crops with hail and locusts, killed their cattle with disease, and afflicted the people with painful boils, loathsome vermin, and thick darkness. And when the cup of iniquity was full, Pharaoh hardened his heart even further. Through Moses, God adressed Pharaoh: "Israel is my firstborn son, and I told you, 'Let my son go, so he may worship me.' But you refused to let him go; so I will kill your firstborn son" (Exodus 4:22–23; cf. 11:4–8). Now He determined to break the iron will of Egypt with one last plague. The specter of death was to fly by night over the land, interrupting the line of inheritance, bringing tragedy to every home where Jehovah was not feared and obeyed.

Although their redemption was at the door, the Israelites were not automatically exempt from this last plague. God tempered His final judgment on Egypt with mercy and perfect provision—the substitution of a life for a life. The Lord said:

On the tenth day of this month each man is to take a lamb for his family, one for each household. . . . Take care of them until the fourteenth day of the month . . . slaughter them at twilight . . . take some of the blood and put it on the sides and tops of the doorframes of the houses. . . . I will pass through Egypt and strike down every firstborn . . .The blood will be a sign for you on the houses where you are; and when I see the blood, I will pass over you. No destructive plague will touch you when I strike Egypt. (Exodus 12:3, 6–7, 12–13)

The verb "pass over" has a deeper meaning here than the idea of stepping or leaping over something to avoid contact. It is not the common Hebrew verb, *a-bhar*, or *gabhar*, which is frequently used in that sense. The word used here is *pasah*, from which comes the noun *pesah*, which is translated Passover. These words have no connection with any other Hebrew word, but they do resemble the Egyptian word *pesh*, which means "to spread wings over." Arthur W. Pink, in his book *Gleanings in Exodus*, sheds further light on this:

The word is used . . . in this sense in Isa. 31:5: "As birds flying, so will the Lord of Hosts defend Jerusalem; defending also He will deliver it; and passing over (*pasoach*, participle of *pasach*) He will preserve it." The word has, consequently, the very meaning of the Egyptian term for "spreading the wings over and protecting"; and *pesach*, the Lord's Passover, means such sheltering and protection as is found under the outstretched wings of the Almighty. Does this not give a new fullness to those words, "O Jerusalem! Jerusalem! . . . How often would I gave gathered thy children together, as a hen does gather her brood under her wings?" (Luke 13:34). . . . And this term *pesach* is applied (1) to the ceremony . . . and (2) to the lamb . . . the slain lamb, the sheltering behind its blood and eating of its flesh, constituted the *pesach,* the protection of God's chosen people beneath the sheltering wings of the Almighty. . . . It was not merely that the Lord passed by the houses of Israelites, but that He stood on guard protecting each blood-sprinkled door! ["The Lord . . . will not suffer the destroyer to come in" (Exodus 12:23.)][2]

God includes everyone in the death sentence in Exodus 11:5: "Every firstborn son in Egypt will die." God must do the just thing because He is God, but He balances His righteousness with His loving mercy. He decrees judgment for all sin and all sinners; then He provides a way of escape, a *kiporah,* or covering. While rain falls on everyone, those who have an umbrella do not get wet. For those who seek His way to satisfy the demands of His Law, God provides the blood of the lamb as a covering.

Israel's redemption began that night behind the safety of blood-sprinkled doors. It was a night of horror and grief for anyone who had foolishly disregarded God's command. It was a long night of vigil mixed with hope for the obedient. Perhaps wails of anguish could be heard from outside as the grim reaper of death went from house to house. Perhaps there was only thick, ominous silence. The people knew that terror and death lay outside that door, which they dared not open until morning.

It was a night of judgment, but the substitutionary death of the Passover lamb brought forgiveness to God's people. It washed away 430 years of Egypt's contamination. The blood of the lamb protected them from the wrath of the Almighty. Its roasted flesh nourished their bodies with strength for the perilous journey ahead. They ate in haste, loins girded, staff

Christ in the Passover

in hand, shoes on their feet, prepared to leave at any moment at God's command. In that awe-filled night of waiting, they experienced Jehovah's loving protection even in the midst of His fierce judgment. They gained a trust that was deep enough to see them through another black night soon to come. They would stand at the edge of the churning waves of the Red Sea with the entire host of angry Egyptians at their backs, and they would trust the words of Moses: "Stand firm and you will see the deliverance [of] the LORD" (Exodus 14:13).

The Lord often works on behalf of His people when things look darkest. In the words of the psalmist, "weeping may remain for a night, but rejoicing comes in the morning" (Psalm 30:5). And so the morning came, and with it joy and freedom.

Out of His mercy, and because He would keep His covenant, the Lord rescued Israel. The seed of Abraham must not forget their commitment to the Holy One of Israel, and they must not forget His promises. They must remember that He brought them out of Egypt with a strong hand and with His outstretched arm.[3]

God speaks in terms of human experiences . . .

Chapter Three

GOD'S
OBJECT LESSON

The Lord's redemption of Israel needed to be stamped on the minds and hearts of future generations. How can a people best remember their history? Books and scrolls may only capture the interest of the scholarly, and in time, words can lose their meaning. God, the master Teacher, devised the perfect method. He commanded the annual reenactment of that first Passover night, a ceremony that would appeal to the senses. Even as we teach children today through object lessons, Jehovah used everyday acts of seeing, hearing, smelling, tasting, and touching to teach holy truths to His people.

THE LAMB

God began His object lesson to Israel with the Passover lamb. First, the people had to single out from their flocks the handsomest, healthiest looking yearling. An animal of this age, just approaching the prime of its life, was frisky and winsome. Then the family had to watch it carefully for four days before the Passover to make sure it was perfect in every way. During this period of close observation, they fed and cared for the lamb and grew accustomed to having it around. By the end of the fourth day, it must have won the affection of the entire household, especially the children. Now they all must avoid its big, innocent eyes as the head of the house prepared to plunge in the knife. While meat was a treat in ancient times, how could they enjoy eating their lamb's flesh? The lesson was painful. God's holiness demands that He judges sin, and the price is costly. But He is also merciful and provides a way of escape (redemption).

The innocent Passover lamb foreshadowed the One who would come centuries later to be God's final means of atonement and redemption:

THE PASSOVER LAMB WAS MARKED FOR DEATH

In Isaiah 53:7 is the prophecy that the Messiah will be led as a lamb to the slaughter. First Peter 1:19–20 says Jesus was foreordained to die before the creation of the world.

THE PASSOVER LAMB WAS TO BE PERFECT

According to Deuteronomy 15:21, only that which is perfect can make atonement. Jesus the Messiah presented Himself in public ministry for three years and showed Himself perfect in heart and deed. Even Pilate found no fault in Him. Hebrews 4:15 says that He was tempted (tested) in all points, yet was without sin. First Peter 1:19 describes Him as a Lamb without blemish or spot.

THEY ROASTED THE PASSOVER LAMB WITH FIRE

In Scripture, fire is symbolic of God's judgment. The prophet Isaiah foretold that the Messiah would bear the sins of many, be wounded for sins not His own, be stricken with God's judgment, and be numbered with transgressors. As Jesus the Messiah suffered the fire of God's wrath and judgment, He cried out from the cross: "My God, my God, why have you forsaken me?" (Matthew 27:46). Second Corinthians 5:21 says: "God made him [Christ] who had no sin to be sin for us , so that in him we might become the righteousness of God."

NOT A BONE OF THE PASSOVER LAMB WAS BROKEN

The Roman soldiers did not break the legs of Jesus the Messiah as they did the legs of the other two men crucified beside Him.

Redemption through the death of the Passover lamb was personal as well as national. Even so, salvation must be a personal event. In the King James version of the Bible, we see a progression in how the lamb is described. In Exodus 12:3, the commandment is to take *a* lamb—a nebulous, unknown entity, nothing special. In Exodus 12:4, God says *the* lamb. Now He is known, unique, set apart. Finally, in Exodus 12:5, God specifies, "*Your* lamb shall be without blemish." Each soul must appropriate the lamb for himself. Arthur Pink quotes Galatians 2:20 to apply this to faith in the Messiah: "The life which I now live in the flesh I live by the faith of the Son of God [the Messiah], who loved me, and gave himself for me."[4] The New Testament refers to Jesus the Messiah more than thirty times as the Lamb of God. Faith and trust in His sacrifice make a person or a nation belong to God.

The Bitter Herbs

They are to eat . . . with bitter herbs. (Exodus 12:8)

Jehovah told the Israelites to eat the Passover lamb with bitter herbs. The first symbolism that comes to mind is the obvious one—the hardships which the Israelites endured under the whips of Pharaoh's taskmasters. But there is a deeper lesson as well. The bitter herbs are a reminder that the firstborn children of the people of Israel lived because the Passover lambs died. God created us humans to gain life through death, to receive physical sustenance from the death of something that once was alive, be it plant or animal. Even so, the believer in the Messiah Jesus receives new life through His death as the Lamb of God.

Besides death, bitterness in Scripture also speaks of mourning. Zechariah 12:10 prophesies that one day Israel as a nation will weep and be in bitter mourning for her Messiah, as when one mourns for an only child who has died. God says in Zechariah 13:9 that He will bring Israel through the judgment of fire and refine her even as silver and gold are refined. Then Israel will proclaim, "The Lord is my God," and in that day "the LORD will be king over the whole earth" (Zechariah 14:9).

The Unleavened Bread

That same night they are to eat the meat roasted over the fire . . . and bread made without yeast. (Exodus 12:8)

The next symbol in God's object lesson is the unleavened bread. The children of Israel ate the Passover lamb with bitter herbs and unleavened bread, then they were to eat no leaven for a full seven days afterward (the Feast of Un-leavened Bread). The symbolism goes deeper than the haste of the departure from Egypt.

Leaven in the Bible is almost always a symbol of sin.[5] The putting away of all leaven is a picture of the sanctification of the child of God. Cleansed, redeemed by God's lamb, the true believer must put away the sinful leaven of the old life before redemption.

In teaching His people this truth, God did not leave them to grapple with abstractions. God speaks in terms of human experiences. Leaven was something that every wife, every cook, used in everyday life. The feel, the smell, the effects of leaven had obvious meaning.

The Hebrew word for leaven is *chometz*, meaning bitter or sour. It is the nature of sin to make people bitter or sour. Leaven causes dough to become puffed up so that the end product is more in volume, but not more in weight. The sin of pride causes people to be puffed up, to think of themselves as far more than they really are.

The ancient Hebrew women used the sourdough method of leavening their bread. Before forming the dough into loaves ready for baking, they would pull off a chunk of the raw dough and set it aside in a cool, moist place. When it was time to bake another batch of bread, they brought out the reserved lump and mixed it into the fresh batch of flour and water to leaven the next loaves (again setting aside a small lump of the newly mixed dough). Each "new genera-tion" of bread was organically linked by the common yeast spores to the previous loaves of bread. The human race bears this same kind of link to the sin nature of our first father, Adam.

Often people excuse themselves for bad behavior or wrong attitudes by saying, "I'm only human." But being "only human" means we share a sinful nature with all humanity. Jesus spoke of leaven, or yeast, as false doctrine and hypocrisy (Matthew 16:11–12; Mark 8:15; Luke 12:1; 13:21).

The apostle Paul in 1 Corinthians 5:6–8 (KJV), spoke of leaven as malice and wickedness. He said, "Purge out therefore the old leaven, that ye may be a new lump [a new person], as ye are unleavened [cleansed]. For even Christ our Passover is sacrificed for us."

On the other hand, Paul described the unleavened bread as sincerity and truth. The Hebrew word *matzo* (unleavened) means "sweet, without sourness." The unleavened bread typified the sweetness and wholesomeness of life without sin. It foreshadowed the sinless, perfect life of the Messiah, who would come to lay down His life as God's ultimate Passover Lamb. In Passover observances after the cessation of the Temple sacrifices, the matzo (unleavened bread) took on added significance when the rabbis decreed it to be a memorial of the Passover lamb.

Thus, for the Hebrews, the putting away of all leaven symbolized breaking the old cycle of sin and starting out afresh from Egypt to walk as a new nation before the Lord. They did not put away leaven in order to be redeemed. Rather, they put away leaven *because* they were redeemed. This same principle applies to the redeemed of the Lord of all ages. Salvation is of grace "not by works, so that no one can boast" (see Ephesians 2:8–9).

THE BLOOD ON THE DOOR

Take a bunch of hyssop, dip it into the blood in the basin and put some of the blood on the top and on both sides of the doorframe. Not one of you shall go out the door of his house until morning. (Exodus 12:22)

Several times Scripture mentions a special mark that will secure exemption from destruction for those who fear the Lord. One such text is Ezekiel 9:4–6; two others are found in Revelation 7:2–3 and 9:4.

When Egypt's judgment was imminent, God commanded the sons of Israel to mark the doors of their dwellings with the blood of the Passover lamb. This blood painted on the doors set apart the houses of those who believed and obeyed God from the houses of those who did not.

The "basin" mentioned in Exodus 12:22 is not like containers used today. It is taken from the Egyptian concept of *sap*, meaning the threshold or ditch which was dug just in front of the doorways of the houses to avoid flooding. The people placed a container in the ditch to prevent seepage. The Israelites killed their Passover lambs right by the doors, and the blood from the slaughter automatically ran into the depression of the basin at the threshold. When they spread the blood with the hyssop brush, they first touched the lintel (the top horizontal part of the doorframe), then each side post (the vertical sides.) In doing this, they went through the motions of making the sign of a bloody cross, the prophecy of another Passover sacrifice to come centuries later. Thus, the door was "sealed" on all four sides with the blood of the lamb, because the blood was already in the basin at the bottom. Arthur Pink sees this as a picture of the suffering Messiah Himself: "Blood above where the thorns pierced His brow, blood at the sides, from His nail pierced hands; blood below, from His nail pierced feet."[6]

We see further symbolism in the words of Jesus, when He said: "I am the gate; whoever enters through me will be saved. He will come in and go out, and find pasture" (John 10:9). The Israelites went in through the blood-sealed door on that first Passover night and found safety. Protected and redeemed by the sacrificial blood, they went out the next morning and began their journey toward the good pasture, the land of promise. We who are redeemed by the true Passover Lamb find safety in Him from God's judgment, and, because of Him, we look forward to a future, eternal haven in the very presence of the Almighty, in the city whose "architect and builder is God" (Hebrews 11:10).

*The Passover celebration, or the neglect of it,
was a thermometer indicating the
community's spiritual condition . . .*

Chapter Four

EARLY OBSERVANCES
OF PASSOVER

After being delivered from the plague of death by the blood of the Passover lamb, the children of Israel greeted the dawn of their redemption with new trust. The night before, they had been timid slaves cowering behind locked doors. Now they threw open their doors and windows to the morning sun and rejoiced in their deliverance. Awed that the power of the Almighty had protected them from the angel of death, they were ready to follow His servant Moses.

That very morning, the Egyptians, fearful of Jehovah's further wrath, begged the Hebrews to leave the country immediately. There was no time to prepare food for the journey, so the Israelites bound up their unleavened dough, still in the kneading bowls, and strapped it to their backs. With this meager supply of food, they set out from Egypt with their wives, little ones, aged, flocks, and all they possessed. They left nothing behind, and their livestock were weighed down with the riches pressed upon them by their frightened Egyptian neighbors.

Four hundred and thirty years earlier, seventy people had come into the land of the pharaohs with Jacob. This day a mighty throng went out. The Bible records that six hundred thousand men left Egypt. Their mothers, wives, and children surely swelled their numbers to almost two million. This newly formed nation would wander in the desert for forty years. A whole generation would grow old and die before they entered Canaan, the land that flowed with milk of goats and the honey of figs. God had left instructions about remembering His provision of escape from Egypt:

> This is a day you are to commemorate; for the generations to come you shall celebrate it as a festival to the LORD—a lasting ordinance. (Exodus 12:14)

> When you enter the land that the LORD will give you as he promised, observe this ceremony. And when your children ask you . . . tell them, "It is the Passover sacrifice to the LORD, who passed over the houses of the Israelites in Egypt and spared our homes when he struck down the Egyptians." (Exodus 12:25–27)

> It is a night to be much observed . . . of all the children of Israel in their generations. (Exodus 12:42 KJV)

> On that day tell your son, "I do this because of what the LORD did for me when I came out of Egypt." (Exodus 13:8)[7]

The word "observed" used in Exodus 12:42 (KJV) comes from the Hebrew root *shamar*, which means "watch." Like the people of Israel on that first Passover, they were to keep watch on every year on the Passover night of remembrance. It was to be a memorial forever.

To the early Hebrew fathers, a memorial was more than a grave marker or a milestone to indicate time or space. They used the memorial to remember or authenticate important events. Throughout the book of Genesis, Abraham, Isaac, and Jacob built altars or placed markers at the sites where God had appeared to them. These markers stood as reminders of God's promises to the seed of Abraham: to make of them a great nation, to give them a land, and to make them a blessing to all people.

God commanded the annual memorial of the Passover observance so that His people might reflect regularly upon all that He had done for them. When they would come into the Promised Land and partake of its goodness, they were to remember the Lord. They were to rehearse and retell the events of the great redemption of their ancestors who had yearned for freedom from slavery. They were to rejoice in past and present blessings and look forward to what God would yet do for and through them.

God gave specific regulations for their celebration:

1. All the congregation of Israel must keep the Passover (Exodus 12:47).
2. They must not allow any stranger to eat the Passover, that is, no one who was uncircumcised or outside the covenant (Exodus 12:43–45).
3. Only one lamb per house was allowed. More than one family could gather, as long as they came together

under one roof and took none of the meat outside the house (Exodus 12:3–4, 46).

4. They must eat the Passover sacrifice entirely in one night, not leaving any for the morning (Exodus 34:25).
5. They must put away all leaven from their tables and from their houses for seven days (Exodus 13:6–7).
6. They must offer the blood of the sacrifice without leaven (Exodus 34:25).
7. They must not break any bones of the Passover lamb (Exodus 12:46).
8. They must sacrifice the Passover only at the place appointed by God (Deuteronomy 16:5–6).
9. All males of the congregation must appear before the Lord at Passover time (Exodus 23:17; 34:23).

Only those who were of the household of faith could participate in the Passover festival of redemption. If Gentile visitors or servants wanted to share in the memorial, they first had to become Jews, that is, undergo circumcision, which would make them part of the covenant. The fulfillment of God's promise to Abraham—that in his seed all the nations of the earth would be blessed—has done away with that kind of restriction. Now all those who trust in Israel's Messiah for redemption belong to the new covenant of grace. They have undergone circumcision of the heart (Jeremiah 31:31–33; Romans 2:28–29) and are eligible to celebrate the new memorial. As Paul wrote to the Ephesian believers, the Gentiles, who at one time were "excluded from citizenship in Israel and foreigners to the covenants of promise," who by faith in Jesus, the Lamb of God, became "no longer foreigners and aliens, but fellow citizens with God's people and members of God's household" (Ephesians 2:12, 19).

CHRIST in the Passover

Now, instead of exclusion, there is inclusion. As Israel celebrated the memorial of redemption from Egypt, now there is an even greater redemption to commemorate: forgiveness of sin and new life through Jesus, God's perfect Lamb. Because of Christ's sacrifice, all people, Jews and Gentiles, only need to submit to a spiritual circumcision of the heart to be brought under the new covenant redemption.

After those instructions concerning Passover in the book of Exodus were written, the Scriptures record only one observance during the forty years of the wilderness journey. Numbers 9:1–14 describes a Passover celebration on the fourteenth day of the first month in the second year after the departure from Egypt, "just as the LORD commanded Moses" (v. 5). At that time God made provision through Moses for a second or "minor Passover," as rabbinical commentaries later called it. Anyone who was ceremonially unclean or who had been away on a journey on the fourteenth day of the first month, the regularly appointed time, could instead celebrate the Passover on the fourteenth day of the second month.

No other Passover celebration is recorded in the Bible until we read of the children of Israel's coming into the land of Canaan. This lapse was probably due to the problem of circumcision. Joshua 5:5 seems to indicate that they suspended the law regarding circumcision during the wilderness journey, possibly because of the dangers of infection. Then, as the older generation died in the dessert, no one was left who had been circumcised, and no one was eligible to carry out the Passover memorial.

In Joshua 5:7–9, the first thing that the Lord commanded Joshua when the Hebrews came into the land was the circumcision of all males who had been born in the wilderness. Thus, the Lord "rolled away the reproach of Egypt" (v. 9), and the children of Israel kept the Passover on the fourteenth day of the month in their new homeland.

However, after Joshua's death Passover observances waned again (2 Kings 23:22). The people who once heard God's thundering voice from the holy mountain listened to the voice of temptation and fell into idolatry. While Passover was observed during the time of Samuel, David, and Solomon, and occasionally after the united kingdom of Israel divided, on the whole, the Israelites were not seeking to follow God's commandments concerning Passover or anything else. But their hearts would be stirred by revival.

The writer of 2 Chronicles tells of two such revivals and the Passover celebrations that immediately followed. One happened in the reign of King Hezekiah (726 BC) and the other during the reign of King Josiah (621 BC).

Second Chronicles 30 records the Passover of Hezekiah. The king ordered the priests and Levites to cleanse and rededicate the Temple and to sanctify the altar. He sent a letter to all the people in Israel, Judah, Ephraim, and Manasseh to come up to the house of the Lord in Jerusalem to celebrate the Passover. As a result, a great revival took place, and the people kept the Feast of Unleavened Bread with much gladness and singing. The Scriptures say there was not such great joy in Jerusalem since the days of Solomon, and therefore they kept the feast for an additional seven days after the first seven. The Lord heeded their prayers and healed their backsliding.

Second Chronicles 35:1–17 tells of the Passover celebration after the reform and revival under King Josiah. Verse 18 of this chapter records that there had been no Passover celebration of this magnitude since the days of Samuel the prophet: "none of the kings of Israel had ever celebrated such a Passover."

Then, in 586 BC, the king of Babylon destroyed the Temple and carried the people away into exile. In Babylon, the children of Israel were once again strangers in a foreign land. Perhaps their circumstances reminded them of their ancestors' bondage in Egypt. But if this prompted them to keep the Passover, we have no record of how they observed it.

After the return from Babylon, the Israelites rebuilt the Temple and "on the fourteenth day of the first month, the exiles celebrated the Passover" (Ezra 6:19). At that time, not all the Jewish people returned to the land. Some stayed in Babylon, where they had built businesses and made new lives for themselves; others migrated and formed small Jewish communities throughout the civilized world. Even among those who did not return, ancient records show us that observing the Passover became a permanent part of Jewish religious life. Those outside of Jerusalem could not sacrifice the Passover lamb unless they made a pilgrimage there, but they did keep the other two important precepts of the holiday: they purged all leaven from their households, and they ate unleavened bread for seven days.

Thus, throughout the history of the children of Israel, the Passover celebration, or the neglect of it, was a thermometer indicating the community's spiritual condition. When the rule of certain kings gave rise to self-indulgent living and a decline in morals, the people's religious commitment was affected. In the intertestamental period (c. 400 BC to AD 50), persecution and oppression by Gentile conquerors spurred the Jewish people to renewed spiritual fervor, for they valued what they were in danger of losing. *The Book of Jubilees* written in the second century BC tells us about journeys made to Jerusalem to celebrate the feast and describes both the formal procedures and the expressions of praise and joy.

Each succeeding generation added customs and traditions to embellish the Passover celebration. Nevertheless, the underlying theme remained the same: the Almighty had brought freedom and new life to His people, Israel, through His supernatural power.

The memory of that miracle-filled redemption occupied the people's minds and hearts at Passover—its most tangible, visible symbol being the solemn sacrifice of the Paschal lamb at the Temple in Jerusalem. As the Jews celebrated Passover during those years of uncertainty and change, hopes were high that soon the Messiah would come to vanquish the Roman oppressor, just as God had brought deliverance from the wicked Egyptian pharaoh.

They delighted in songs, storytelling,
word games, riddles, the exchange of news,
and long discussions on religious matters . . .

Chapter Five

PASSOVER IN
THE TIME OF CHRIST

At Passover, a stream of humanity ribboned the highways leading into first-century Jerusalem. Devout Jews poured in from distant corners of the world to worship Jehovah on the mountain of His holiness. If at all possible, those Jews who lived within a few days' journey came up to Jerusalem three times a year: at Passover, at Pentecost, and at the Feast of Booths. But for many who lived far from Jerusalem, a pilgrimage at Passover was the fulfillment of a once-in-lifetime dream.

Weeks before the holiday, the trickles began—from Asia Minor, from Egypt, from Africa, from Italy, from Greece, from Mesopotamia.[8] Whether the first part of the journey was by boat or by land, no one ever went *down* to Jerusalem.[9] The holy city sat like a crown 2,610 feet above sea level, and the Temple was its brightest, most prominent jewel. In order to reach this destination, all travelers first had to go through the surrounding valleys, and then, in what felt like a symbolic journey toward holiness, they climbed upward to Jerusalem.

By mule, in ox cart, and on foot they came—families, schools of disciples following their teachers, and solitary travelers banded together in caravans for safety from robbers and wild animals. Their voices rang out through the valleys below in echoes of the Pilgrim Psalms and Songs of Ascent:

As the deer pants for streams of water, so my soul pants for you, O God. (Psalm 42:1)

How lovely is your dwelling place, O LORD Almighty! My soul yearns . . . for the courts of the LORD. (Psalm 84:1–2)

I rejoiced with those who said to me, "Let us go to the house of the LORD." Our feet are standing in your gates, O Jerusalem. (Psalm 122:1–2)

How good and pleasant it is when brothers live together in unity! (Psalm 133:1)

Praise the LORD, all you servants . . . who minister by night in the house of the LORD. (Psalm 134:1)

The number of permanent residents in Jerusalem in Jesus' time was about six hundred thousand. A conservative estimate of the vast multitude of Passover pilgrims that came to the city is about two million. Those who came from afar arrived at least a week or two in advance, because anyone coming from a country outside of Israel could not worship in the Temple without undergoing seven days of ritual purification.

At Passover, Jerusalemites and their visitors, despite vastly differing cultural backgrounds, rejoiced in the unity of their Jewishness. People were reunited with blood kin whom they had not seen for months or even years. Pilgrims without relatives or friends in Jerusalem found themselves being welcomed as family members into homes where they had never been, by people they had never met.

The earliest to arrive camped around the Temple site, as the tribes had once camped around the tabernacle in the wilderness, but this space was limited. The area surrounding Jerusalem was too rocky and hilly for pitching large numbers of tents, so many residents opened their homes to the visiting worshipers. They were forbidden by custom to charge rent, but hosting was a joyful obligation. Their exotic visitors had tales to tell of distant places and cultures. Usually the host and his household were given hospitality gifts, things that brought the sight, smell, and feeling of adventure.

During the four weeks before Passover, the synagogues and academies placed much emphasis on teaching and reinforcing the holiday's meaning. Jerusalem was filled with excitement and expectancy, and all the citizenry prepared for the festivities and the influx of visitors. Members of the Sanhedrin busied themselves with arrangements for the repair of roads and bridges leading into the city. Housewives sewed new garments for everyone in the household and cleaned vigorously. Vendors in the marketplaces expanded their stock in anticipation of the increased business. Even the beggars, huddling at the gates in their rags, dreamed of a season of bounteous compassion and generosity, prompted by the worshipers' piety.

One preparation custom involved whitewashing the tombs

around the city. The people of that time buried their dead in caves and sealed off the openings with large stones so that wild animals would not desecrate the bodies. But the numerous caves around Jerusalem were used for other purposes as well. People kept livestock in caves and used them for shelter.[10] It was possible that a traveler, seeking refuge at night or during a spring rainstorm, might blunder into a burial site. Since this contact with a dead body would defile him, he would have to undergo an elaborate ritual cleansing before being able to worship in the Temple. For this reason, they marked the tomb entrances and surrounding areas with a white, chalky material to warn people. This whitewash wore off and needed replacing periodically, and it was the custom to do these repairs at the Passover season.

These freshly painted tombs provided Jesus with the imagery He used to rebuke the Pharisees in Matthew 23:27–28. They thought of themselves as a repository of truth and light, but there was an infectious spirit of death to their self-righteousness. Their outward piety looked good and right, but people needed to be warned away from their teachings, because following them would only lead to death and decay.

Jerusalem was a commercial city as well as the seat of government and religion. The most common meeting grounds to befriend strangers and offer them hospitality were the gates of the city, the marketplaces, and the synagogues.

Their nearly 360 synagogues were not characterized by their neighborhood locations, but rather they consisted of people with like interests, like trades, and in like stages of life. Thus, there were synagogues of potters, synagogues of tentmakers, synagogues of Greek-speaking Jews, and so forth.

The synagogue was not only a place of learning. It took the place of the community center, the grain storehouse, the hiring hall, and the fraternal lodge. Here tradesmen met their foreign counterparts and exchanged knowledge, and artisans were introduced to new methods and designs. Passover was a time for seeking new apprentices, since some who came early for the holiday joined the craftsmen in their trades.

In the marketplaces, the tables and blankets of wares were larger than usual and held a more colorful variety of goods. Many travelers brought goods they could sell in order to obtain the local currency. Food vendors supplied extra commodities, often of a more luxurious nature than their everyday products, to meet the increased needs and festive mood. Here was a rare spice and exotic ointment; there, a familiar homespun made intriguingly different by the startling brilliance of some new dye, a new kind of carpenter's tool, a cleverly designed potter's wheel, a finely crafted silver wine goblet, or an elaborately concocted food to tease the nostrils.

At Passover, Jerusalem was filled with itinerant rabbis and teachers, who often brought along their whole academies. These scholars enriched the homes of their hosts with the benefit of their knowledge and inspiration. All rabbis were learned in matters of the Law, and at Passover they had the opportunity to compare notes and share interpretations and precedents of both Jewish and Roman law.

It was a time of hustle and bustle for all kinds of people. Business contacts and deals were made. Servants undergoing the Passover rituals indentured themselves for life to their masters' households. Those of the priestly class brushed up on Temple customs—after all, their sons might have an opportunity to sing with the Levitical choir, or they might find a bride of equal station. It was a matter of prestige to marry a daughter of Jerusalem, for those women were not of peasant stock and often came from priestly, scholarly, or merchant families.

Passover season gave people the opportunity to sit in the marketplace or at the gates and enjoy conversation. Jewish people of that time usually did not play physical games for recreation and entertainment, as did the Greeks and Romans. Rather, they delighted in songs, storytelling, word games, riddles, the exchange of news, and long discussions on religious matters. One might learn of battles, of uprisings, of scandals among rulers, of a particularly lenient tax collector at one of the tollgates, or of a wealthy merchant seeking a son-in-law.

Amidst the bustle and din, a change in the wind might carry down the sound of the Temple services—the music, the chanting of the priests. People then turned their eyes upward to the towering structure high atop Mount Moriah, which dominated the landscape in all directions. They saw the smoke from the sacrifices curling upward against the sky, and they remembered their real purpose for being there: the worship of Jehovah, the true and living God. That was the scene; those were the sights, the sounds, the smells that greeted Jesus and His disciples as they entered Jerusalem the week before the Passover.

A crucial part of the final preparations of that last week before the feast was the removal or storing away of all leaven in each Jewish home. That included bread, all leavening agents, and any cereals or grains that had the capacity of becoming leavened. There was also the ceremonial cleansing of the pots and utensils in the house.

On the night before Passover eve, a search was made for any leaven that might have been overlooked. At that time, the head of the household went through the house, inspecting it with a lighted candle or lantern in complete silence. If he found any leaven, he disposed of it or locked it away where it would not be touched until after the Passover and the eight days of unleavened bread, which followed. Then the head of the house repeated an ancient prayer, which Orthodox Jews still use today: "All leaven that is in my possession, that which I have seen and that which I have not seen, be it null, be it accounted as the dust of the earth."

Jewish tradition believes there is a reference to this searching for leaven in Zephaniah 1:12 (KJV).[11] God said in that verse: "I will search Jerusalem with candles," meaning He would search out the leaven of sin and destroy it. The apostle Paul probably had this search for the leaven in mind when he said in 1 Corinthians 5:7 (KJV): "Purge out therefore the old leaven [sin], that ye may be a new lump, as ye are unleavened [cleansed from sin]. For even Christ our passover is sacrificed for us."

At the same time people throughout the city were preparing their homes, special attention was being given to the central subject of the feast, the Paschal lamb. In obedience to Scripture, a representative of each household chose their sacrifical lamb on the tenth of Nisan. If someone bought a lamb outside the Temple, he had to take it to be inspected by the priests and declared without blemish or spot; or he could buy a lamb already certified by the priests within the Temple complex. Most people bought lambs in the Temple, knowing from bitter experience that the priests could almost always manage to find some minute imperfection on any animal brought in from the outside.[12]

On the fourteenth of Nisan, the slaughter of the Passover lambs took place. The crowds of worshipers entered by company into the Temple's outer courtyard. The priests chose "companies" of no less than ten people, no more than twenty. There was a lamb for each group, which they would later eat as their ceremonial meal. The Levities killed the lambs at the signal of the silver trumpets sounded by the priests.

Then they removed the fat and burned it. They caught the blood of the sacrifices in bowls, which two rows of priests passed along to be poured out at the base of the altar.

While all this was happening, the Levitical choir chanted Hallel, the recitation of Psalms 113 to 118. The congregation joined the liturgy by repeating the first line of each psalm after the Levites sang it. They also chanted the words *Hallelu Yah* (praise ye the Lord) at the end of every line. When the priests came to Psalm 118, the congregation repeated verses 25 and 26 (KJV):

> Save now, I beseech thee, O LORD [Hoshiah-Na, or Hosanna]: O LORD, I beseech thee, send now prosperity. Blessed be he that cometh in the name of the LORD.

These are the very words that rang out through the streets of Jerusalem a week before the crucifixion as Jesus rode into the city on a donkey in fulfillment of Zechariah 9:9. The two disciples sent by Jesus to prepare the Passover heard them again as they stood in the court of the priests to kill their lamb. As their memory of that joyful acclaim mingled with the reality of the death scene before them, one wonders whether they began to understand what the Master had been trying to tell them when He said:

> "We are going up to Jerusalem, and everything that is written by the prophets about the Son of Man will be fulfilled. He will be handed over to the Gentiles. They will mock him, insult him, spit on him, flog him and kill him." (Luke 18:31–32; cf. Matthew 20:18–19; 26:2; Mark 9:31–32; 10:33–34)

*Jesus taught them that
it was not ceremonial rites but acts of
faith and love that were most important . . .*

Chapter Six

THE ANCIENT SEDER AND THE LAST SUPPER

THE ANCIENT SEDER

Some Pharisees of Jesus' day regarded the oral traditions of the ancient sages as being of equal authority with the *Torah*, the written law of God. Orthodox Jews today still believe that God Himself delivered these oral traditions to Moses and that they were then passed by word of mouth to each succeeding generation. Those earliest known rabbinical commentaries were edited and compiled into one authoritative body of religious thought called the *Mishnah* sometime between AD 100 and 210. The Mishnah covers every aspect of Jewish religious life and depicts the customs, traditions, and observances at the time of Christ.

According to the Mishnah, the basic obligations of the Passover observance are the same as those commanded in the book of Exodus. In Pesahim 10:5, the Mishnah quotes Rabbi Gamaliel as saying:

> Whoever does not make mention of the following three things on Passover has not fulfilled his obligation; namely, the Passover sacrifice, unleavened bread and bitter herbs. The Passover sacrifice because the Holy One . . . passed over the houses of our fathers in Egypt; unleavened bread . . . because our fathers were redeemed from Egypt; the bitter herb . . . because the Egyptians embittered the lives of our fathers in Egypt.

By the first century, the Passover observance included several new customs in addition to the obligations described in the Torah account. Already, a set form of service called the *seder*, meaning "order of service," was in use. The celebrants reclined at the table in the Babylonian custom of free people. (Slaves stood in attendance while their masters ate.) The ceremony included ritual hand washings and set prayers. The celebrants drank four cups of wine as a symbol of joy. Oral tradition contained in the Mishnah said that even the poorest person must drink the minimum four cups, even if he had to sell himself to do labor or borrow money to buy the wine. The Passover wine was red and mixed with water. From a passage in the Mishnah (Pesahim 7:13), it would appear that the wine was warm because the water was heated. If this is true, then the wine also graphically represented the blood of the Passover lamb.

Beside the roasted Paschal lamb, the bitter herbs, and the unleavened bread, other ceremonial foods were on the table.[13] Salt water or vinegar was used for dipping the bitter herbs once. Then there was *charoseth*, a sweet mixture of apples and nuts. This was eaten together with the bitter herbs and the unleavened bread. They ate no dessert since the lamb was to be the last solid food tasted. But after the destruction of the Temple in AD 70, an after dish known as the *aphikomen* came into use. This wafer of the unleavened bread represented the Temple Paschal sacrifice that was no longer possible without the Temple.

In the time of Christ, at the outset of the feast the head of the household (the host) recited *kiddush* over the first cup of wine. This prayer consecrated the occasion and the meal to God. The words, if not exactly those used today, were very similar.

> Blessed art Thou, O Lord our God, who hast created the fruit of the vine. . . . Blessed art Thou, O Lord our God who hast sustained us and enabled us to reach this season.

After drinking the cup, next came the ceremonial washing of hands by the host. At this point a servant brought in a portable table of food, and the first dipping of food took place. This was the raw vegetable, usually lettuce, which was considered bitter herb. The head of the feast dipped the vegetable into salt water or vinegar and passed it around to all at the table. It was a common practice for beginning a meal, and it can be likened to hors d'oeuvres or appetizers. But here, as in all things that were eaten and done on that night, there is a deeper symbolism, which is discussed later.

After dipping the bitter herbs, the food was removed from the table. Then the host poured the second cup of wine, but the participants did not drink it yet. Removing the food without eating the main course (the Paschal lamb) was an unusual procedure intended to raise curiosity.

The next step in the ritual would then follow naturally.

This was the asking of questions by the youngest son so they could obey the command of God to "tell your son."[14]

The questions in ancient times were:

1. Why is this night different from all other nights? On all other nights we can eat bread or matzo. Why tonight only matzo?
2. On all other nights, we can eat any kind of herbs. Why tonight bitter herbs?
3. On all other nights we don't dip herbs we eat into anything. Why tonight do we dip twice?
4. On all other nights we eat meat roasted, stewed, or boiled, but why tonight only roasted meat?

Then the father gave a synopsis of Israel's national history, beginning with the call of Abraham out of idolatry and ending with Israel's deliverance from Egypt and the giving of the Law. After that, the food was brought back. The Father continued the service by explaining the lamb, the bitter herbs, and the unleavened bread. Then they sang the first part of the Hallel (Psalms 113 and 114) and drank the second cup of wine.

They then washed hands the second time, as an act of respect for the unleavened bread they were about to eat. The host broke one of the wafers and pronounced the blessings over bread. There were two blessings. One was a prayer of thanksgiving to Him who brings forth bread from the earth; the second was thanksgiving for the commandment to eat unleavened bread. Traditionally, these blessings were spoken over bread that had first been broken in order to show humility, remembering that the poor had only broken bits of bread to eat. The host gave a piece of this broken bread, dipped in bitter herbs and the sweet charoseth mixture to each person.

After the bitter herbs and the bread, they ate the Paschal lamb. If the lamb was too small for everyone to have enough, they also ate the *Haggigah* (a holiday peace offering). But, in that case, they ate the Haggigah first, so that the Passover lamb would be the last food they ate that night. The host poured the third cup, they all recited the after-meal blessing and chanted another over the wine, and then everyone consumed the third cup.

Next, they recited the second portion of the Hallel (Psalms 115–118) and drank the fourth cup. The seder came to an end with a closing song or hymn, which began: "All Thy works shall praise Thee, Jehovah, our God," and concluded: "From everlasting to everlasting Thou art God, and beside Thee, we have no King, Redeemer, or Savior."

THE LAST SUPPER

The Passover ordinance commemorated Israel's historical redemption from Egyptian slavery. God gave it as an object lesson to be observed by all those who counted themselves as being made free by His power. But equally important was the hidden symbolism of a greater future redemption, which would free from sin all those who cried out to God. It would be a redemption for all people, Jews and Gentiles, to bring them into a new and eternal relationship with their Creator and with each other through the King Messiah. The Jewish people yearned and prayed for that redemption as they groaned under the yoke of Rome. Yet when the fulfillment of the promise was at the door, few recognized it.

The Teacher from Nazareth came into their midst, exciting the masses with His words of wisdom spoken with authority. He healed the sick, opened the eyes of the blind, caused the lame to walk, and showed miraculous power over the physical laws of nature. Many hoped that He was the one to free the nation from its oppressors and set up God's kingdom on earth, but they expected Him to do it by military might. Expectations ran high as Jesus entered Jerusalem that last week before the Passover. After all, the original Passover was the key to Israel's redemption from Egypt and the subsequent giving of His holy Law. Since many important events in Israel's history were connected to Passover season, many thought God would send the Messiah at this time.

Both the faithful and the scoffers watched Jesus carefully those few days before the Passover. They saw Him overthrow the money tables in the Temple. What would He do next? Would He tell them that He, indeed, was the long-awaited Messiah? Alas, they were disappointed. He only continued to teach, and many things He said were not comforting to hear.

Now it was the eve of the Passover celebration. Jesus sent two of the disciples, Peter and John, to prepare for the ritual meal. They found a room as He had instructed them and performed all the necessary preliminaries. When all was ready, Jesus reclined with the Twelve at the Passover table to eat their last meal all together. Here, on the eve of His death, He showed them the full meaning and symbolism of the Passover memorial.

The picture of that Last Supper comes into sharper focus when some of the Scripture recording the Last Supper is compared with some of the ancient elements of the Passover service:

THE KIDDUSH:

> After taking the cup, he gave thanks and said, "Take this and divide it among you. For I tell you I will not drink again of the fruit of the vine until the kingdom of God comes." (Luke 22:17–18)

THE FIRST WASHING OF HANDS:

> He got up from the meal, took off his outer clothing, and wrapped a towel around his waist . . . and began to wash his disciples' feet. (John 13:4–5)

> (This was followed by the bitter herbs dipped in salt water; table of food removed; second cup of wine poured; ritual questions asked and answered; table of food brought back; explanation of lamb, bitter herbs, and unleavened bread; first part of Hallel; second cup taken; second washing of hands; one wafer of bread broken; and thanks over bread recited.)

BROKEN PIECES OF BREAD DIPPED IN BITTER HERBS AND CHAROSETH AND HANDED TO ALL:

> Then, dipping the piece of bread, he gave it to Judas Iscariot, son of Simon. . . . "What you are about to do, do quickly," Jesus told him . . . As soon as Judas had taken the bread, he went out. (John 13:26–27, 30)

> (The Paschal meal eaten; hands washed a third time; third cup poured.)

BLESSING AFTER MEALS:

The Lord Jesus, on the night he was betrayed, took bread, and when he had given thanks, he broke it and said, "This is my body, which is for you; do this in remembrance of me." (1 Corinthians 11:23–24)

BLESSING OVER THIRD CUP (CUP OF REDEMPTION):

In the same way, after supper he took the cup, saying, "This cup is the new covenant in my blood; do this, whenever you drink it, in remembrance of me." (1 Corinthians 11:25)

(Third cup taken; second part of Hallel recited; fourth cup poured and taken.)

CLOSING SONG OR HYMN:

When they had sung a hymn, they went out to the Mount of Olives. (Matthew 26:30)

The first hand washing by the host set him apart from the rest of the company. It showed that he was the most important person at the table. In washing the disciples' feet, Jesus used this part of the regular ritual to teach a lesson of humility and love. He knew that the Father had given Him all things; even the wind and the sea obeyed Him. Yet He humbled Himself and acted out the role of a slave. Jesus taught them that it was not ceremonial rites but acts of faith and love that were most important. He even washed the feet of Judas!

It was during the ceremony of dipping the bread into the bitter herbs that Jesus said, "one of you will betray me"

(Matthew 26:21). Peter motioned to John, who was reclining so that he leaned on Jesus' bosom, to ask who the betrayer was. Jesus whispered His answer: "It is the one to whom I will give this piece of bread when I have dipped it in the dish" (John 13:26).

One may wonder why John did nothing to stop Judas. But it must be remembered that the statement could have been taken to mean any one of them at the table. They all partook of the sop, although Judas probably received it first. After the bread, Judas went out into the night to finish his Satan-inspired work. Because he left before eating the Passover, he had, in effect, excommunicated himself from the congregation. Neither did he have any part in the new memorial that came after supper.

The bread that Jesus broke to dip in the bitter herbs was not the bread of which He said, "This is my body" (Matthew 26:26). The bread He compared to His body came after He gave thanks at the end of the meal; then He broke it and gave it to them, saying, "This is my body given for you; do this in remembrance of me (Luke 22:19; cf 1 Corinthians 11:24).

Not only the words were shocking. It was a very unusual act, for after supper no other food was to be eaten. Here Jesus instituted the new memorial. He was telling the disciples in cryptic terms that after His death, the Paschal lamb would no longer have the same significance. It was the memorial of historical redemption of the Exodus, but only a shadow of the ultimate redemption soon to come. He was about to become the better sacrifice, to die once, for all (Hebrews 9:14–15, 23–26). Looking to the time when Israel would be left without an altar and without a sacrifice, He used the *aphikomen* (after dish) for the first time to represent not only the Paschal lamb, but His own body!

And then He took up the wine again and prepared the third cup for them: "In the same way, after the supper he took the cup, saying, 'This cup is the new covenant in my blood, which is poured out for you'" (Luke 22:20). He who was the great "I AM" was there in the flesh. He had stood before them on other occasions saying, "I am the way and the truth and the life" (John 14:6); "I am the gate" (10:9); "I am the light of the world" (8:12); "before Abraham was born, I am" (8:58). Now He had one more great truth to impart to those who could receive it. He was telling them, in effect: "I am the true Passover Lamb who will be offered up for your redemption. This warm red wine that you drink tonight as a symbol of joy, is to remind you evermore of My life's blood, which will be poured out as an atonement for you!"

The Gospel accounts of the Last Supper mention only two of the four seder cups—the first and the third. According to early Jewish tradition, these two were the most important. The first cup was special because it consecrated the entire Passover ritual that followed. But the Mishnah states that the third cup had two names: the "cup of blessing," because it came after the blessing or grace after meals, and the "cup of redemption," because it represented the blood of the Paschal lamb. It was of *this* cup that Jesus said, "This is my blood of the new testament [covenant]" (Matthew 26:28 KJV). It is this cup of blessing that Paul mentions in 1 Corinthians 10:16: "Is not the cup of thanksgiving for which we give thanks a participation in the blood of Christ? And is not the bread that we break a participation in the body of Christ?"

PASSOVER AND EASTER

Almost all the early Christians were Jewish. They celebrated the resurrection of Jesus at Passover time and called it *Pascha*. (Later it was mistranslated Easter.) They continued to celebrate the resurrection in this manner during the time of the first fifteen bishops of Jerusalem, who were of Jewish descent.[15] The bishops sent out Paschal epistles every year to notify the Christians when Passover would fall according to the Jewish lunar calendar (i.e., the fourteenth day of Nisan). By AD 325, however, paganism and anti-Jewish sentiment had invaded the Church. Emperor Constantine, who presided over the Council at Nicaea, prohibited Christians from continuing to celebrate the resurrection at exactly the same time as the Jewish Passover.[16] Still, to this day, the two holidays are celebrated at approximately the same time, both being based on the lunar calendar.

The death and resurrection of Jesus the Messiah are forever interwoven with the Passover and its symbolism. The Passover lamb spoke of the Lamb of God who was to come. The redemption from Egypt foreshadowed the greater redemption that Jesus would bring. To deny these truths of Scripture is not only to miss a rich heritage, but to cut oneself off from God. A person who would purpose to do so is like the person who climbs a tree and then tries to chop it down while seated in its branches!

Some well-meaning, albeit misinformed, Christians today have accused Jewish Christians of "Judaizing" and "Galatianism" because they choose to celebrate Jewish holidays and remember their cultural roots. Nothing is further from reality. The Jewish believer in Jesus finds deep significance in God's commandments concerning the festivals and customs of His people, Israel. In the new light of salvation in Christ, these things are relevant to our faith, not in opposition to it. We gain no merit with God in observing the festivals, but if we ignore them, we miss the blessings of an appreciation of the heritage that is the cradle of our faith and subsequent salvation.

The apostle Paul dealt with this subject when he wrote by the moving of the Holy Spirit in Romans 14:5–6, 10:

One man considers one day more sacred than another; another man consider every day alike. Each one should be fully convinced in his own mind. He who regards one day as special, does so to the Lord. He who eats meat, eats to the Lord, for he gives thanks to God; and he who abstains, does so to the Lord and gives thanks to God. . . . You, then, why do you judge your brother? Or why do you look down on your brother? For we will all stand before God's judgment seat.

And again, he wrote in Colossians 2:16–17:

Therefore do not let anyone judge you by what you eat or drink, or with regard to a religious festival, a New Moon celebration or a Sabbath day. These are a shadow of the things that were to come; the reality, however, is found in Christ.

We must again look into the home, the family unit,
to see and know the Passover of today . . .

Chapter Seven

PREPARING FOR THE CONTEMPORARY PASSOVER

As long as the second Temple stood, Jerusalem remained the hub of Jewish life. However in AD 70, Roman armies leveled the great house of worship. The prophetic words of Jesus came to pass.[17] Only rubble and ashes covered the Temple site.

Exiled, without an altar, and without a sacrifice, the Jewish people felt a deep need to remember and rehearse the great things Jehovah had done for them in days past. They clung to the hope that once again He might do marvelous things for them.

It is fitting that this hope continues to burn in the hearts of God's chosen people, for "God's gifts and his call are irrevocable" (Romans 11:29). Against all odds, through centuries of oppression and struggle, the Jewish people survived. They nurtured the memories of the past and fervently looked for future deliverance.

Families and communities bore the responsibility of keeping a spark of faith alive in the darkness and despair of exile. The holidays and traditions were links in the chain of survival. So the celebration of "The Season of our Deliverance" took on new meaning and setting.

The people of the Diaspora embellished and added to the required ritual of the Passover in order to intensify and reinforce the holiday's meaning. They wrote special songs with memorable melodies and rhythms. Celebrants reclined on cushions to promote a sense of freedom and relaxation. Lamps and candles were used so they could see the festival's familiar elements in greater brightness. Even the sense of taste was involved as they adopted foods from other cultures to enhance the holiday table with savory dishes. While they continued to drink the four cups of wine to symbolize gladness, the main course of the feast was conspicuously missing!

What can Passover be without the Passover lamb? It is like a wedding without the bridegroom. The holiday that is today called Passover is really the eve of the Feast of Unleavened Bread. Even as far back as Bible times, the observances of Passover and the Feast of Unleavened Bread were referred to by both names and were often treated as one holiday.[18] However, the remembrance of redemption from death through the blood of the lamb is overshadowed by emphasis on the redemption from Egyptian slavery and thoughts of national liberty.

How, then, do Jewish people celebrate Passover today? We will not find the answer in the synagogue. It is not in the pages of the well-worn prayer books, nor is it in the parchment scrolls of Holy Writ encased in mantles of scarlet and blue velvet. The first Passover rituals took place in individual homes. There they were, Hebrew families gathered around the table for a meal—a meal that was to become the epic symbol of the past redemption and future hope. We must again look into the home, the family unit, to see and know the Passover of today.

PRELIMINARIES

The Jewish wife tackles her spring cleaning with a holy zeal. This is because Passover comes in the spring, in the month of Nisan, also called *Abib*. She is preparing to obey the command in Exodus 12:19: "For seven days no yeast is to be found in your houses." Do the walls need paint, carpets need shampooing, cupboards need arranging? Wait until just before Passover! The straw broom of ancient days has given way to the vacuum cleaner, but the end is still the same. Every scrap of bread, every cookie crumb, every bit of yeast, every speck of baking powder or other leavening agent must go. Families must also banish from the home all grain products that have the capability of becoming leavened. If they have too many of these costly staples to throw away, the rabbis have provided a remedy. They store all the items in one place in the house. This can be a high, out-of-the-way shelf or, better yet, an unused room. Then they find a Gentile friend, who is not bound by the laws of Israel, to buy title to all the leaven. The purchase price is a token amount, usually a dollar or two. Now, technically, the leaven is no longer in the possession of the Jewish household, though it remains locked away in the house. After the seven days of the holiday, the Gentile friend will sell back all the leaven (for the same low price, one would hope!).

Now it is the thirteenth of Nisan, the day before the Passover celebration. The house is hospital clean. Even the floors gleam and sparkle. The rays of the late afternoon sun stream in through windows, so spotless they look invisible.

Not in any corner, nor under any piece of furniture, is there so much as a speck of dust or a crumb of leaven. But the house is not yet clean.

As in ancient times, the ceremonial search for the leaven, called *Bedikat Chametz,* is led by the man of the house. The ceremony and the prayer remain much the same as they were two thousand years ago. Some rabbinical authorities say that he must search every room; others say only those rooms that would normally have food in them.

For the search, the head of the house takes with him a child to hold the lighted candle and some strange cleaning equipment: a wooden spoon, a feather, and an old cloth napkin. He searches upstairs and downstairs, in the attic, in the basement, and in all the rooms until he comes to the last room. His wife knows beforehand which room this will be. Just so he will not have said the prescribed prayer in vain, she has placed a few crumbs in a highly visible spot where he can easily find them. They may be crumbs from the morning toast, but they are something unclean! He points the feather at the offending material and sweeps it into the wooden spoon. Then he wraps spoon, feather, and crumbs in the old napkin and pronounces the words of the ancient formula: "Now I have rid my house of leaven."[19] The next morning he joins the other men of the Jewish community at a designated ritual bonfire. They all toss in their bundles of leaven and return home ready for the Passover.

After the house is ritually clean, the everyday dishes are put away and out come special dishes that are used only at Passover. If the home is too poor to afford special dishes, the old dishes must be ritually cleansed. This is a complicated process. The rule is that the metal utensils like pots and pan must be heated until red hot; cutlery must be placed in boiling water; glazedware must be soaked in cold water. Because unglazed pottery is too porous and cannot be cleansed, it must be put away until after the holiday.

THE SEDER TABLE

At sundown on the fourteenth of Nisan, everything is ready for the beginning festivities. The children are as scrubbed and shiny as the furniture, and everyone is wearing new clothes. Hunger-teasing aromas float out of the steamy kitchen and fill the house, making it difficult to concentrate on other matters. But it is not yet time for food.

The stage is set in the dining room for the ceremonial part of the meal. The table is covered with fine linen and the candles are lit as though in preparation for the Sabbath. Indeed, the holiday is considered a Sabbath, being designated a "holy convocation" in the Bible. But this is no ordinary table with ordinary place settings.

In a prominent place on the table sits the seder plate, the focal point of the whole seder service. This seder plate is a large, segmented brass dish. It is specially designed with divisions for each of the six symbolic foods, but a family may use an ordinary large serving plate without partitions. The symbolic foods on the plate are much the same as those used on seder tables for the past several hundred years.

First on the plate we see the roasted shank bone of a lamb (or sometimes a chicken neck instead). The name of this symbol is *zeroah*, which means "arm" or "shoulder." It represents the Paschal sacrifice, which is no longer possible. The zeroah also speaks of the outstretched arm of the Lord, by which He freed His people from Egypt.

Next, we see a hard-boiled egg that has been roasted to a brown color. It name on the seder plate is *betzah*, which literally means "egg." However, the symbolic name for the egg is *haggigah*, meaning the holiday sacrifice that was made in Temple times. Many interpret this egg as a symbol of new life and hope and triumph over death (resurrection). Before the regular meal, hard-boiled eggs are sliced and given to all persons at the table. They dip the eggs in salt water, which represents tears, and eat them to portray mourning over the destruction of the Temple.

The seder plate holds three kinds of bitter herbs. Two of these we recognize as being bitter. One, a piece of whole horseradish root, is called *chazereth* in Hebrew.[20] The other is freshly ground horseradish, *maror* in Hebrew. The third bitter herb, surprisingly, is a piece of lettuce, parsley, or celery. It is designated *karpas*, and it is the first food that will be eaten at the seder. The ancients considered lettuce and endive to be bitter herbs. The Talmud states: "Just as lettuce at first tastes sweet and then bitter, so did the Egyptians treat our ancestors. At first they settled them in the best part of the land, . . . but later they embittered their lives" (Yerushalmi Pesahim 29). In the contemporary Passover service, the karpas is not usually considered a bitter herb. Rather, it is thought of as a symbol of life because it is usually a green of some sort. However, Jewish people of some cultures do use radishes or raw potato instead. These substitutions remain in keeping with the ancient concept of using bitters for the first course.

Last on the seder plate we see a sweet, brownish mixture of chopped apples, nuts, raisins, cinnamon, and wine, called *charoseth*. Jewish people who come from Middle Eastern and Mediterranean cultures, where they do not grow apples but have an abundance of figs, use chopped figs instead of apples. Charoseth is symbolic of the mortar or red clay of Egypt, which the children of Israel used when they were forced to make bricks for Pharaoh. The question may be asked: "If this mixture represents the bitter labor of Egypt, why is it sweet to the taste?" "Ah," says one sage, "when we knew that our redemption drew nigh, even the bitterest of labor was sweet!" Charoseth is not commanded in Scripture. Nevertheless, like the eating of the hard-boiled eggs, it dates back to very ancient times.

In addition to the contents of the seder plate, three more items are essential to the Passover table: the unleavened bread, the wine, and the *Haggadah.*

The unleavened bread (*matzo*) of ancient times was flat, round, and irregular in shape. Likewise, the hand-baked matzo of today, used by stricter sects of Judaism, is round and somewhat irregular in shape. However, most modern matzo is machine-made and square, measuring about seven inches. These flat, bland, crackerlike wafers are marked with even rows of tiny holes. The perforations, which are put in to prevent excessive bubbling of the dough, cause uneven browning, which produces a striped appearance. In an earlier chapter we examined the symbolism of the unleavened bread as a type of picture of the sinless Messiah Jesus.[21] The appearance of the stripped and pierced matzo brings to mind two verses of Scripture that help to complete the picture: "With his [Messiah's] *stripes* we are healed" (Isaiah 53:5 KJV); and "They [Israel] will look on me, the one they have *pierced*, and they will mourn for him" (Zechariah 12:10).

The unleavened bread on the table is encased in a special container called the *matzo tash*. The matzo tash is a square, white, silk bag that is divided into three compartments for three matzo wafers. If the family does not own one of these bags, three pieces of matzo must be stacked on a plate, each wafer separated with a napkin; then the three wafers are covered with another cloth. According to Jewish tradition, these three matzo wafers symbolize unity. Contemporary

Judaism gives no set interpretation of this unity, but there are several popular theories. One school of thought declares it to be the unity of the fathers of Abraham, Isaac, and Jacob. Another thought is that the unity represents the unity of worship in Israel, that is, the priests, the Levites, and the rest of the congregation. A third idea is that it is the unity of crowns—the crown of learning, the crown of the priesthood, and the crown of kingship. Another Jewish source explains that two of the pieces of matzo represent the traditional loaves set out in the ancient Temple during the festival day, and the third is symbolic of Passover.[22] We will explore yet another interpretation later as we look at the modern seder.

Also at the seder table, beside each place setting are small wine goblets—small because four times they will be filled with sweet, red Passover wine during the seder. The custom of drinking four cups of wine dates back to ancient Temple times. The Mishnah teaches that, according to two authorities, Rabbi Yohanon and Rabbi Benayah, these four cups correspond to the four verbs in Exodus 6:6–7, describing God's redemption: I will *bring* you *out*; I will *free* you; I will *redeem* you; I will *take* you to be My people.

Two of the wine goblets at the table are usually larger and more ornate than the rest. They have silver, intricate pictures of the Bible history crafted into the metal. One of these goblets sits at the head of the table for the ruler of the feast; the other occupies a prominent place at the foot of the table, before an empty chair. It awaits the lips of Elijah, who, according to Malachi 4:5, is to announce the coming of the Messiah. The prophet is the invited guest of honor at every seder, for, should he come, it would indeed be the most festive of Passovers! The Messianic hope prevails more strongly at Passover than at any other time, for Midrashic tradition says: "Nisan is the month of redemption; in Nisan Israel was redeemed from Egypt; in Nisan Israel will again be redeemed" (Exodus Rabbah 15:12).[23]

The last item to notice on the table is a large, decorative book called the Haggadah. This book more than covers the host's dinner plate. Bound in a royal blue, velvety cover, it is inscribed with gold lettering and illustrated with many colorful reproductions of ancient art. Next to each person's place setting is a much smaller, plain, paperbound edition of the same book. The participants will need these to follow along during the service. The Haggadah not only tells what to do at the seder, but also when, how, and why. Haggadah is Hebrew for "telling," or "showing forth." It is the same root used in Exodus 13:8: "On that day *tell* your son." We find the same connotation in the Greek, where the apostle Paul, in describing the Last Supper, writes: "For whenever you eat this bread and drink this cup, you *proclaim* the Lord's death until he comes" (1 Corinthians 11:26).

Our modern Haggadah is based on ancient writings in the Mishnah about Passover. These fragments date back to the second century. The first full record we have of the Haggadah is contained in a section of an old prayer book called seder, or *siddur*, which was edited in the ninth century by Rabbi Amram ben Sheshnah. The Haggadah finally emerged as a completely separate book in the thirteenth century. Much of the ritual and thought contained in even the latest versions goes back as far as Maccabean and second Temple times.

These, then, are the unique foods and accoutrements on the Passover table. But before the ritual meal itself is examined, there is yet another unusual feature to capture our attention. On each chair around the table there is a pillow. Most are sofa pillows, but often one or two bed pillows are used as well since everyone must have one. All at the table tonight will recline or sit at ease during the ceremonial meal, for once we were slaves in Egypt, but now we are free. Once we ate the Passover in fear and haste, but tonight we eat in leisurely comfort and safety. We celebrate redemption. We rejoice in liberty.

Lighting of the holiday candles separates the sacred from the mundane

The head of the house raises his cup as he recites
the blessing over the cup, the fruit of the vine

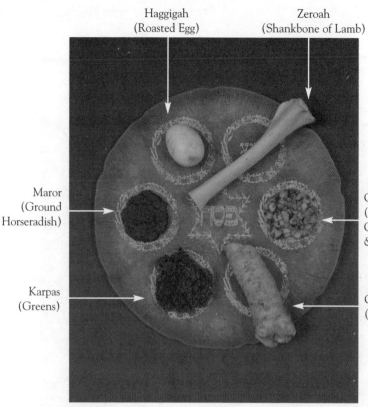

Haggigah
(Roasted Egg)

Zeroah
(Shankbone of Lamb)

Maror
(Ground
Horseradish)

Charoseth
(Apple,
Cinnamon,
& Nut Mixture

Karpas
(Greens)

Chazereth
(Bitter Root)

Seder Plate

The cup of Elijah, the haggigah, and the matzo tash

The youngest child asks the traditional Ma Nishtanah (Four Questions)

The charoseth (apple mixture) is placed on a piece of matzo
and eaten by all around the Passover table

"Let us bless Him whose food we have eaten."

Chapter Eight

THE MODERN SEDER

In Jewish homes, the lighting of the holiday candles separates the sacred from the mundane, the Sabbath of rest from the week's cares. Tonight the flame casts a halo over the holiday table, inspiring a sense of holiness. It lends a soft patina to the silver, and the flickering glow is mirrored in the eyes of the seated company. Savory aromas from the kitchen mingle with the scent of the hot wax, the grapey smell of wine, and the acrid fumes of freshly ground horseradish. An air of festivity reigns, tempered by solemn anticipation.

The father or grandfather of the family conducts the Passover seder. For this special occasion, the leader of the feast is wearing a long, white outer garment of cotton or silk, called a *kitel*. The kitel is worn by Orthodox Jewish men at Passover and a few other special times. It is also a burial garment.[24] This wide-sleeved ceremonial robe is a symbol of purity, reminiscent of Temple times when no one could participate in the sacrifices unless he was in a state of Levitical purity. It also reminds us of the high priest's white robe and the robe of righteousness that God has promised to give His elect (Isaiah 61:10; Revelation 6:11; 7:9). On his head, the leader of the feast wears a tall, white, silk head covering shaped like a crown, portraying that on Passover night a man is king and religious leader over his household.[25]

All eyes now turn expectantly to the leader as he stands and opens his Haggadah. He raises his wine glass for all to see and chants the *kiddush*, the prayer of sanctification that ushers in all Sabbath days and most of the Jewish holidays. This blessing expresses thanksgiving to God for choosing Israel and for giving feasts and holidays to His people. On Passover night a special blessing is added for the commandment to commemorate the redemption from Egypt. The most widely recognized portion of this prayer is: "Blessed are thou, Lord our God, King of the Universe, Creator of the fruit of the vine." Upon the close of this benediction, everyone at the table sips from the first cup of wine, called the *cup of sanctification*. This cup of sanctification consecrates the ritual meal.

Next, a small towel and a silver bowl filled with water is brought to the table. This ceremonial washbasin contains only about a cup of water. The leader dips his fingertips into the bowl and dries them with the towel in preparation for handling the food. He picks up the *karpas* (celery, parsley, or lettuce) from the seder plate and hands a small portion to each participant. Everyone recites together: "Blessed art thou, Lord God, King of the Universe, who creates the fruit of the earth." And everyone dips the greens into salt water and eats. At ancient Greek and Roman banquets, this was the traditional beginning for a formal meal. Their Hellenistic culture influenced Jewish custom and practices during the formative stages of standardizing the seder. Contemporary thought endows the ritual with added symbolism: the greens represent life, which is often immersed in tears, represented by the salt water.

The host now turns his attention to the unity, the three wafers of unleavened bread. He bypasses the top wafer, takes out the middle wafer, and breaks it in half. He puts one of the halves back into the unity. Then he wraps the remaining piece of this middle matzo in a white napkin or puts it into a special, white, silk bag. While the children cover their eyes, he hides or "buries" that portion of the middle matzo, usually beneath one of the pillows or under the tablecloth. This buried or hidden wafer of unleavened bread now has a name, *aphikomen*. We will see the aphikomen later in the Passover service.

The ritual that follows is very old. We know this because the prayer is in Aramaic, the language used in Israel during the time of the second Temple. To this day it is read in Aramaic, not Hebrew. The host uncovers the unleavened bread again, holds up the plate, and everyone recites: "This is the Bread of Affliction which our ancestors ate in the land of Egypt. Let all who are hungry come and eat. Let all who are in need come and celebrate Passover." Then they include phrases that must have been added after the destruction of the Temple: "This year we are here: next year in the land of Israel! This year we are slaves: next year free people! Here again, as with the cup set out for Elijah, we see the Messianic hope expressed. Although we are free from Egyptian slavery, we are slaves. When the Lord brings us back to Zion in the days of the Messiah, we will be truly redeemed, truly free!"

Now the wine glasses are filled, and the youngest child at the table asks the traditional four questions, similar to those of ancient times:

1. Why is this night different from all other nights? On all other nights we can eat bread or matzo. Why tonight only matzo?
2. On all other nights, we can eat any kind of herbs. Why tonight bitter herbs?
3. On all other nights we don't dip herbs we eat into anything. Why tonight do we dip twice?
4. On all other nights we can eat either sitting up straight or reclining. Why tonight do we all recline?

The last question about reclining is a relatively late addition to the original questions. It may have been as a replacement for the question referring to the Paschal lamb, which was asked while the Temple and the sacrifices remained: "Why do we eat only meat which is roasted?"

The father or grandfather replies with the prescribed answer in the Haggadah, taken from Deuteronomy 6:21 and 26:8: "We were slaves of Pharaoh in Egypt . . . so the LORD brought us out of Egypt with a mighty hand and an outstretched arm."

From this introductory statement proceeds the reading of the whole epic of redemption from the Haggadah. The Mishnah describes this answer as "beginning with shame and ending with glory" (Pesahim 10:4). The narrative combines Bible history and rabbinical commentary. It includes God's calling Abram out of idolatry, the hardships of the Hebrews in the land of Egypt, the punishment of the Egyptians, and the dividing of the Law. The climax is the recital of the ten plagues that God poured out on the Egyptians. With the mention of each plague, all participants dip or pour out one

CHRIST in the Passover

drop of wine from his or her wine goblet into a small saucer. This saucer, not the goblet, is known as the cup. When the saucer is filled with ten drops of wine, it is called the *cup of iniquity*, a term symbolic of God's judgments. Now is posed the rhetorical question: "Is it for this [the judgment] that we praise God?" The answer follows: "No, for God loved the Egyptians even as He loved us. But it is for God's infinite mercies that we praise Him."

This sets the stage for a happy song recounting the numerous acts of love and mercy that God bestowed upon Israel. The name of the song is one Hebrew word, *dayenu*, meaning "it would have been sufficient." At the end of every line of the song comes the one-word refrain, "Dayenu," sung about ten times with much gaiety and handclapping. The song ends with the spoken words:

Then how much more, doubled and redoubled, is the claim the Omnipresent has upon our thankfulness! For He did take us out of Egypt and execute judgments . . . and justice . . . [did] tear the sea apart for us, . . . satisfy our needs in the desert, . . . give us the Sabbath [and] . . . the Torah [Law], . . . bring us into the land of Israel, and build us the House of His choosing to atone for all our sins.

Now, in obedience to the ancient admonition of Rabbi Gamaliel, the host makes special mention of the three crucial ingredients of the Passover: the Passover sacrifice (symbolized by the shank bone on the seder plate), the bitter herbs, and the unleavened bread (matzo). He explains each item, holding up the bitter herbs and matzo. However, he does not lift up the shank bone, lest what is only the symbol of the Passover lamb be given the significance of a real sacrifice, which is forbidden. Then he adds these words:

In every generation let each man look on himself as if *he* came out of Egypt. As it said: "On that day tell your son, 'I do this because of what the LORD did for *me* when I came out of Egypt'" [see Exodus 13:8].

This text is based on the teaching of the Mishnah (Pesahim 10:5) that the Exodus and redemption are not to be taken only as history; each Jew is to consider the experience as personal. (Even so, those of us who are spiritually redeemed by Jesus, the true Passover Lamb, see Him as being sacrificed for each of us, individually and personally, although the actual event happened two thousand years ago.)

Now the company raises the wine glasses in a toast of thanksgiving to the goodness of God and proclaims: "Let us then recite before Him a new song: Hallelujah!" They put the glasses down without drinking and recite Psalms 113 and 114, the first portion of the Hallel, which literally means "praise." Then they raise the wine glasses once again, repeating the ancient prayer of Rabbi Akiba, probably written just after the destruction of the Temple.

> Blessed art thou, O Lord, . . . who redeemed us . . . and has brought us to this night . . . So, O Lord, . . . bring us to other festivals, . . . happy in the building of thy city . . . And there may we eat of the sacrifices and the paschal offerings, whose blood will come into the walls of thy altar for acceptance. Then shall we give thanks to thee with a new song, for our redemption and the liberation of our soul. Blessed art thou, O Lord, Redeemer of Israel. Blessed art thou . . . Creator of the fruit of the vine.

This is the signal for drinking the second cup of wine, called the *cup of praise*.

CHRIST *in the Passover*

Following the drinking of the second cup, they pass around the basin of water. All recite the special prayer for ceremonial handwashing and wash their hands.

The head of the feast now breaks off pieces of unleavened bread and distributes them to all at the table. They recite together the prayers of thanksgiving for the commandment to eat unleavened bread, and they eat a morsel of the matzo.

Next, the host dips some of the bitter herb into the sweet charoseth mixture and offers a piece to each participant. Before eating it, they pronounce another benediction, thanking God for commanding the eating of bitter herbs. Any resultant tears are a fitting memorial to the hardships of their ancestors.

The host goes on to make a sandwich of bitter herbs and unleavened bread. He eats it, saying:

In memory of the Temple, according to the custom of Hillel. Thus did [Rabbi] Hillel when the Holy Temple still stood: he used to combine unleavened bread and bitter herbs and eat them together, to fulfill that which is said: "They shall eat it with unleavened bread and bitter herbs."

By this time, some may be a bit droopy-eyed from the warmth of the room, the sips of wine, and the hypnotic flickering of the candles. But most will find themselves jolted into alertness by a mouthful of horseradish. Now the seder plate is set aside and a few people disappear into the kitchen. This is the real cue for everyone to come to life—here come the good things that have been teasing their nostrils all day!

The Passover meal is a banquet. It usually begins with the traditional hard-boiled eggs dipped or flavored with salt water. Then come the appetizers. In Ashkenazi homes (those of northern and eastern European culture), two of the favorite appetizers are chopped liver and gefilte fish. Many people like to use horseradish instead, even when it is not Passover. Then, almost always, there is a matzo ball soup: a rich, clear chicken broth accompanied by fluffy, feather light dumplings made of finely ground matzo and many well-beaten eggs. The main course is usually a stuffed fowl or beef of some kind. Jewish people today traditionally do not eat lamb on Passover, because there is no Temple and no Passover sacrifice. But those of us who are Jewish believers in the Messiah Jesus feel that it is meaningful to eat lamb at our Passover meals in remembrance of the One who came to be the Lamb, whose sacrifice overshadows the sacrifices of all the lambs slain in the Temple (Hebrews 9).

There are many more good things to eat, like salads and vegetables, as determined by the cook's imagination and resourcefulness. For dessert there are dried fruits, nuts, specially baked Passover cookies, sponge cakes, and coconut macaroons—all made without leaven—and imported marzipan and other candies from Israel.

Jewish people of Eastern and Mediterranean descent (Sephardim) have different favorite foods in keeping with their own culture and tradition. Their cuisine often includes tomatoes, eggplant, and fruits like dates, figs, and oranges, which are native to their countries. The only foods never to be found on any Passover table, beside bread or other types of leaven, are pork and shellfish. These are forbidden at all times by Leviticus 11 and Deuteronomy 14 to those Jewish people who are still under the Law.

With dinner at an end, the dessert dishes are cleared away, but the Passover seder is far from finished. Something is missing—the *aphikomen*! The name aphikomen comes from the Greek *epikomios*, meaning "after dinner revelry" or "that which comes last." In ancient times, this was apt to be rather rowdy. Since that type of behavior was totally unsuitable for a religious celebration, the rabbis of old substituted a solemn commemoration of the Paschal lamb. In Temple times, the lamb was the last thing to be eaten; now, in the absence of the sacrificial lamb, the unleavened bread was to represent the Passover sacrifice. The taste of the matzo and the memory of the lamb were to linger in the consciousness of each celebrant.

The children search now for the missing aphikomen, making a little game of it. The adults call out clues as the children search the room: "You're way off base . . . still cold . . . getting warmer!" Soon someone finds it and gives it to the head of the feast with a triumphant grin of anticipation, knowing he or she will receive a reward for it—a small gift or sum of money.

The gaiety and boisterousness of the search give way to solemnity as the ritual of the seder continues. The host unwraps the aphikomen and distributes olive-sized pieces to everyone.[26] All partake of it with quiet reverence. In Western culture, there is no blessing or word spoken. But in the Sephardic or Eastern tradition, they say: "In memory of the Passover sacrifice, eaten after one is sated."

After this, no one may have any more food or drink at the seder other than the third and fourth cups of wine. At this point many Haggadahs include the recital of Psalm 126, one of the Songs of Ascent.

Now that the meal is officially concluded by eating of the aphikomen, the ritual portion of the seder continues with the recitation of the final table grace. At Jewish meals there is a *berachah* (short prayer of thanks) for each food as it comes to the table, but the main prayer always comes after the meal. At the seder, the host now pours the third cup of wine before this prayer. Then he stands and repeats the traditional words in Hebrew: "Gentlemen, let us recite the blessing."

The seated company responds: "May the name of the Lord be blessed from now unto eternity."

The host continues: "Let us bless Him whose food we have eaten."

Then the participants read a lengthy prayer of thanksgiving. Toward the end of this table grace, we hear again the expression of hope in God's final deliverance in the days of the Messiah:

> Take pity, O Lord, . . . on Israel, . . . on Zion the habitation of thy glory and on the kingdom of the House of David, thine anointed. . . . May there rise and come . . . the remembrance of us . . . and our fathers, and the remembrance of the Messiah the son of David, thy servant, . . . and Jerusalem thy holy city . . . and all thy people the House of Israel, . . . on this festival. . . . The Compassionate One—may He send Elijah the prophet (may he be remembered for good) to us that he may bring us good tidings of salvations and consolations.

If Passover falls on a Friday night (the beginning of the Sabbath) they also add the following:

> The Compassionate One—may He cause us to inherit that day which is all Sabbath and repose, in the everlasting life. The Compassionate One—may He find us worthy of the days of the Messiah and of the life of the world to come.

This speaks of that ultimate Sabbath of rest about which Paul is writing in Hebrews 4:9.

CHRIST in the Passover

Immediately following that prayer, the host leads again in the blessing over the wine, and everyone drinks the third cup, commemorating the verse in Exodus 6:6: "I will redeem you with an outstretched arm." This third cup is the *cup of redemption*, also at times called the *cup of blessing*. It is the cup of redemption because, say the ancient commentaries, it represents the blood of the Paschal lamb. Some Haggadahs call it the *cup of Elijah* because it directly follows the prayer for the coming of Elijah. Another reason for that title may be because of what happens next.

The children have been watching Elijah's cup at the foot of the table. In some households, the cup was filled at the beginning of the seder; in others, it is filled now. They squint hard at the dark red contents of the cup. Will Elijah come and drink from the cup? Maybe he is here now, only he is invisible. Did he take a sip? It looks like there is just a little less wine than there was a while ago! Alas, if that is true, it is only due to evaporation. But maybe he is still going to come! Wait and see, but now we must go on with the service.

Jewish scholars think the prayer that comes next, "Pour Out Thy Wrath," originated during the Middle Ages when Jews were severely persecuted for the faith, especially at Passover time. This prayer is not found in the earliest editions of the Haggadah. It calls for God's judgment on the heathen, and it sounds rather harsh. But taken in context with the other prayers given above for the coming of Elijah, it fits into the pattern of thought: "May God send the Messiah, heralded by the prophet Elijah, to vanquish all our enemies and set up His Kingdom of peace."

The leader now sends one of the children to open the door to see if Elijah is coming in answer to the prayers. The words are not prescribed until later in Haggadah reading, but just as the door is being opened, everyone usually exclaims:

"Blessed is he who cometh in the name of the Lord!" The youngsters are wide-eyed with awe as the door slowly creaks open. A gust of cool night air sweeps into the room, but no one is there. Oh well, maybe next year! The child closes the door and comes back to the table.

Next, the host leads the recitation of the second portion of the Hallel, Psalms 115 to 118. These verses are the same as those read when the Temple was still standing. They lead into the Great Hallel, which is Psalm 136. In this well-known psalm, the Levitical choir in the Temple sang out the praises of Jehovah and the great events of Israel's history. At the end of each phrase or line, the congregation responded, "For His kindness endureth forever!"

The earliest commentaries (Pesahim 10:7 of the Misnah) record a "Benediction of Song" after the Hallel. The Talmud, which is a commentary on the Mishnah, teaches in Berakhot 59 that one of these benedictions was the Great Hallel and another was at least some part of a hymn called "The Breath of Every Living Thing." This closing hymn before the fourth and final cup of wine is again a prayer of praise and thanksgiving. It begins: "The breath of every living thing shall bless Thy Name," and ends: "Blessed art thou, O Lord, God and King, who art mightily praised, God of thanksgiving, Lord of wonders, who chooses song and psalm, King, God the life of the world."

Once again, everyone at the table lifts his wine glass and chants the blessing over wine. Everyone drinks from the fourth cup. This last cup of the Passover seder commemorates the verse in Exodus 6:7: "I will take you as my own people."

One of the modern versions of the Haggadah comments very aptly on the fourth cup and the verse it commemorates: "The redemption is not yet complete. The Fourth Cup recalls us to our covenant with the Eternal One, to the tasks that still await us as a people called to the service of God, to a great purpose for which the people of Israel live."[27]

The editors of that particular Haggadah see the purpose of Israel as being "the preservation and affirmation of hope." But we, who are familiar with the promises and prophecies of Scripture, see a greater purpose for Israel—that of one day proclaiming to the whole world that the Messiah is, indeed, Savior and King!

Because of the words, "I will take you to be my people," some call this fourth cup *the cup of acceptance*. Others prefer to call this cup (instead of the third one) the *cup of Elijah*. There is merit to both titles, for Elijah will yet come to herald the redemption that will be complete only when Israel fulfils God's entire plan; that is, when Israel recognizes and proclaims the Messiah (Zechariah 12:10), she will truly be the people of God as foretold in Jeremiah 32:38–40.

And now, at last, with the drinking of the fourth cup, the seder is drawing to a close. Happy songs and festivity often continue afterward late into the night, but the service officially ends with one last prayer for the rebuilding of Jerusalem:

> Concluded is the Passover seder,
> According to its law and custom.
> As we have lived to celebrate it,
> So may we live to celebrate it again.
> Pure One, who dwells in his habitation.
> Redress the countless congregation.
> Speedily lead the offshoot of thy stock
> Redeemed, to Zion in joyous song.
> NEXT YEAR IN JERUSLAM![28]

"Why do we hide the aphikomen
and bring it back later?"

Chapter Nine

THE FIFTH QUESTION

The holiday candles have turned to shallow pools of wax in their festive holders; the savory meal is only a pleasant memory; and the young children are losing their battle against heavy eyelids. The Haggadah is closed and returned to its place on the shelf for another year.

Once again we have rejoiced in the festival of freedom. We have made merry; we have been serious. We have feasted, taken the traditional four cups of wine, sung praises to God, rehearsed the story of His redemption of Israel. We have recalled His promises, and we have discussed the comments of the ancient rabbis. We have heard the four questions, and we have learned what makes *this* night different from all other nights.

Still, other questions remain unanswered —unanswered because they go unasked.

Elijah has not come. The naked bone of the Passover plate confronts us with the knowledge that we no longer have a Passover lamb, nor a Temple for the unified worship of Jehovah our God. Most of us are physically free from bondage, but aren't we still slaves—to our limitations, our faults, our circumstances? And then there is the ultimate question: "Do those questions remain unanswered because we do not care enough to ask them, or because we are afraid to ask them?"

In asking the four prescribed questions at the seder, little children know just what to say. They have been rehearsing those lines for weeks. The words roll off their tongues in Hebrew or Yiddish as easily as their play songs, their names and addresses, or a recitation of their schoolwork. So easily that they need not really think about what they are asking. But what if one of those youngsters were to become curious and interrupt the middle of the Passover service with, "Papa, why do you take out the middle piece of matzo instead of one of the others? Why do we hide the aphikomen and bring it back later?"

These are puzzling questions, since we have no one authoritative explanation of the symbolism of the unity of the three pieces of matzo on the Passover table. None of the given theories about the nature of this unity provides a satisfactory answer to the hypothetical question of why we break the middle matzo.[29]

If the unity is that of the three fathers, why do we break Isaac and not Abraham or Jacob? If it is the unity of worship, why do we break and hide the Levites rather than the priests or the congregation of Israel? Or if it is the three crowns, why do we single out the crown of the priesthood rather than the crown of learning or the crown of the kingship?

Neither Jewish folklore nor rabbinical Judaism has an

adequate answer to these perplexing questions. But there is a plausible explanation. Contemporary Jewish authorities readily admit that the Passover service and the Haggadah evolved through centuries of change, and some portions are older than others. One such Jewish author, Chaim Raphael, in his book A *Feast of History*, suggests that the rituals of the traditional seder "reflect in origin the world in which the Jews found themselves while these ceremonies were being shaped for future generations."[30] Raphael acknowledges the influence of early Greek culture in the format of the Passover meal. He mentions obvious parallels between the dialogues of the Greek philosophers (Plutarch, Athanaeus, Macrobius, and Philo) and the ritual discussions of the Exodus by the ancient rabbis at the Passover seder. In another place in the same book, the author states:

> One has to assume a very fluid state of affairs . . . in the early centuries, even if we see an outline of the seder emerging in the Mishnah. The background of Jewish social life inside and outside Palestine was very unsettled because of political turmoil, the transition from statehood, the proliferation of sects, *and the ambivalent status for a time of the Jewish Christians.*[31]

Admissions such as these by Jewish scholars lend credence to the thought that the many parallels between the entire ritual of the aphikomen and the corresponding symbolism found in the New Testament writings of the early Jewish Christians are too strong to be ignored.

Indeed, the status of the early Jewish Christians was, in the words of author Raphael, "ambivalent." They continued to worship in the Temple and attended the synagogue with their fellow Jews. For a while they were allowed, as a sect of

Judaism, their differences of religious interpretation and emphasis, even as the Sadducees and Pharisees were allowed theirs. When the break finally came, the Jewish believers in Jesus did not abandon the synagogue. Rather, the synagogue expelled the Jewish Christians.

Here, then, is the answer to the puzzling matter of aphikomen. The early Jewish Christians incorporated into their own Passover services the spiritual lessons, customs, and insights taught them by Jesus Himself at the Last Supper. Because these early Jewish Christians at first were considered an acceptable sect of Judaism, some of their customs and interpretations became part of the Passover ritual over time. The use of the aphikomen to commemorate the Passover lamb would have been particularly meaningful to the Jewish people after the destruction of the Temple, although after their break with the Jewish Christians the others might seek to deny the deeper significance of that broken matzo.

At the Last Supper, Jesus made that significance very clear when He instituted the new memorial to commemorate the sacrifice of Himself as the bread of life, the Lamb of God, the ultimate means of redemption for both of Jews and Gentiles. Therefore, the words, "In memory of the Passover Lamb," spoken over the aphikomen in the Sephardic seder,[32] present a double symbolism: The middle wafer *represents* Jesus, the Messiah, who, by His sinless, perfect life, fulfilled the prophetic symbolism of the unleavened bread, and who, by His sacrificial death, fulfilled the prophetic symbolism of the Passover Lamb!

We see, then, in the three pieces of matzo on the Passover table, a truth that remains hidden from most of the Jewish community to this day. That the truth of the unique unity of the eternal God is expressed in the *shemah*, the most widely spoken utterance of faith in all of Judaism, found in

CHRIST *in the Passover*

Deuteronomy 6:4: "Hear, O Israel: The LORD our God, the LORD is one." In the original Hebrew, the word for "one" is *echad*, meaning a composite oneness rather than the absolute number one. This same word, *echad*, appears in Genesis 2:24 to signify that Adam and Eve became "one flesh." It appears again in Ezekiel 37:16–19 to describe the sign of the two sticks that became "one" in the prophet's hand. The three pieces of matzo, then, depict the eternal unity of God: the ineffable *Name*, who appeared to Moses in the burning bush; the Messiah, the Son of David who became flesh that was broken to effect absolute redemption for the entire human race; and the *Holy Spirit*, who guides and directs and empowers the redeemed of the Lord.

At the seder we single out the middle matzo, representing the Messiah, even as He was *foreordained* to die for the sins of the world. We break the middle matzo, signifying His *death*, for He was crucified, even as the psalmist and the prophets foretold in Psalm 22, Isaiah 53, and Daniel 9. We hide the middle matzo signifying *burial*. Just before the third cup of wine, perhaps symbolizing three days, we "resurrect" the middle matzo, just as Jesus the Messiah *rose from the grave* in fulfillment of Job 19:25 and Psalm 16:10. Then all the faithful partake of the middle matzo, signifying a personal, individual part in the everlasting redemption of God, even as Jesus taught:

> I am the living bread that came down from heaven. If anyone eats of this bread, he will live forever. This bread is my flesh, which I will give for the life of the world. (John 6:51)

That new memorial of the death, burial, and resurrection of Jesus the Messiah symbolized the fulfillment of God's plan for redemption for all humanity, which was foreshadowed in the first Passover observance. The Passover celebration of redemption from Egypt still brings joy and gratitude to God's people. But truly blessed are those who appropriate by faith that new memorial, which speaks of the greater, eternal redemption of the soul.

As the Israelites were in bondage to Egypt and needed physical redemption, so all people are in bondage to sin and need to be forgiven and deemed the people of God. This broader redemption is available for all, whether Jews or Gentiles, who will trust in the atoning sacrifice of the Messiah. But it is available only through the Messiah, Jesus. This is the redemption that brings true freedom from the bondage and hopelessness of sin and separation from a holy God.

Just as the redemption from Egypt foreshadowed the greater redemption to come, so many aspects of the Passover celebration point to the ultimate redemption through Jesus, the Lamb of God.

The Passover celebration reminded the children of Israel that once they were slaves to Pharaoh, but now they were free through the power of the Almighty. Those who are redeemed by Jesus the Messiah must remember that once they were slaves to sin, but now they are free from its power.

The slaying of the Passover lamb dramatically depicted to the children of Israel the cost of their rescue and redemption. Those who are redeemed by the death of Jesus the Messiah must remember the terrible cost of redemption— the agony and death of the perfect Lamb of God, who gave His life as an atonement for sin.

Then, in celebrating the Passover, the children of Israel remembered their journey in the wilderness. They recalled the victories Jehovah gave them over their enemies. They remembered that He fed them with manna and gave them water that they might live—that He did not leave them to wander alone, but He led them by His very presence in a pillar of cloud by day and in a pillar of fire by night. He gave them rules to order their lives when willfulness and lack of faith led them to sin. He provided the brazen serpent for their healing and forgiveness, gave them a Sabbath of rest, and finally brought them into the land flowing with milk and honey that was promised to their fathers.

For the eternally redeemed of God, life is a journey through the wilderness of the world. Yet the Lord gives us victory over the Devil, the Enemy of our souls. He feeds us with the Bread of Life and gives us springs of living water. He leads us in the way by the presence of His Holy Spirit, the Comforter who never leaves us. He writes His Law upon our hearts that we may live pleasing to Him, and if we stumble, He forgives our transgressions for Jesus' sake. He has given us the Sabbath of His rest, whereby we wear the robe of righteousness woven by the Messiah's sinless life, so that we need not struggle to achieve impossible standards by our own deeds. He promises us an eternal haven in the life to come in the city whose Builder and Maker is God.

Jehovah gave the Passover memorial to Israel to be a time of praise for past deliverance from Egypt and a time of renewing the hope for future and final deliverance. Those who would not keep the memorial were cut off from the congregation. To be cut off from the congregation was not merely excommunication—it meant physical death.

The second, fuller redemption in God's Messiah does not threaten us with physical death if we forget to commemorate Him who gave His life for us. But putting aside that remembrance does cause severance of fellowship with God and with His people, and neglecting to feed upon the broken Bread of Life starves the new life we have in Him. But if we confess our neglect and unfaithfulness, He is faithful to forgive us and to cleanse us from all unrighteousness. In the words of the apostle:

> Purge out therefore the old leaven, that ye may be a new lump, as ye are unleavened. For even Christ our passover is sacrificed for us: therefore let us keep the feast, not with old leaven, neither with the leaven of malice and wickedness; but with the unleavened bread of sincerity and truth. (1 Corinthians 5:7–8 KJV)

Rejoice in the feast of the Lamb!

*God has prepared a feast of redemption
and joy to which all are invited . . .*

Chapter Ten

COME TO THE FEAST

*Blessed are those who are invited
to the wedding supper of the Lamb!*
(Revelation 19:9)

From the beginning of time, God has wanted to be more significant to us mortals than most would allow. He wants us to enter into the joy He has prepared for us, but we choose more temporal pleasures. He wants to be Lord, but we would rather be in command of our lives. He wants us to trust Him, to rely on Him, and to know that He will bring good into our lives, but we are content to rely on the threadbare traditions of humanity rather than obey His revelation of Himself.

In the land of fools, a fool is crowned king; the king's reign is foolish, and the destiny of his people is to be fooled. The best ways of humanity are rebellious and selfish, and our best thoughts are corrupt. Our destiny is death, and our lives are infected by a fallen world, itself cursed because of our impurity (Genesis 3:17; Romans 8:22).

The Israelites at Mount Sinai trembled in awareness of that impurity. Awed by the rumblings and fire on the holy mountain, they insisted that Moses be a mediator between them and God (Exodus 20:19). Their dread to face God without a mediator was altogether appropriate, for a holy God cannot tolerate sinful humanity.

Jehovah instructed Moses: "Go down and warn the people so they do not force their way through to see the LORD and many of them perish" (Exodus 19:21). No mortal can look upon God. Moses was highly favored of God, but He even spoke to Moses in a thick cloud that hid His glory. When Moses pleaded to see Him, he was told: "You cannot see my face, for no one may see me and live" (Exodus 33:20). But the Lord in His mercy provided a way for Moses to behold Him and yet survive. He hid Moses in a cleft of rock in the holy mountain and allowed him to catch a fleeting view of His glory as He passed by.

The prophets of old were also highly favored of God. He appeared to them only in visions, yet when they glimpsed but a shadow of His being, they felt unworthy and undone. They were devastated, not because they faced an evil tyrant, but because they realized how sin-stained they were by their earthly existence.

The prophet Isaiah, accounted the chief of the writing prophets, must have been one of the most righteous people of his time. But in the presence of God, he cried out in abject despair: "'Woe to me!'" I cried. "'I am ruined! For I am a man of unclean lips, and I live among a people of unclean lips, and my eyes have seen the King, the LORD Almighty'" (Isaiah 6:5). His despair was not due to God's cruelty, but to the realization of how unrighteous his righteousness was. Later he wrote: "All of us have become like one who is unclean, and all our righteous acts are like filthy rags; we all shrivel up like a leaf, and like the wind our sins sweep us away" (Isaiah 64:6).

If the King of heaven were to allow us even a momentary view of Himself, we also would cringe in terror and despair. In His mercy, God does not reveal the infinite beauty of His holiness, lest we see the ugliness of our own sin. While we deserved to be destroyed, God provided a Mediator who spans the gap between our sinfulness and His holiness. Moses himself prophesied of this One who would come to Israel when he wrote Deuteronomy 18:15–19:

> The LORD your God will raise up for you a prophet like me from among your own brothers. You must listen to him. For this is what you asked of the LORD your God at Horeb [Mount Sinai] on the day of the assembly when you said, "Let us not hear the voice of the LORD our God nor see this great fire anymore, or we will die." The LORD said to me: "What they say is good. I will raise up for them a prophet like you from among their brothers; I will put my words in his mouth, and he will tell them everything I command him. If anyone does not listen to my words that the prophet speaks in my name, I myself will call him to account."

This Prophet to come would be like Moses in that He would be the Mediator between God and humanity. He would be the ultimate Prophet who all must heed. Moses spanned the gap between God and Israel for a short time, but he also was only mortal, with mortal flaws and the mortal destiny of death. Being mortal, he could not offer perfect, eternal mediation. In order for there to be perfect mediation, there needed to be some token of eternal value. That Prophet to come was the eternal Christ the Messiah.

By the sacrifice of Himself, Jesus the Messiah accomplished what neither Moses nor the sacrifice of bulls and goats could do. Not only was He the eternal Sacrifice, He was the eternal High Priest who offered that sacrifice. Even as Moses took a higher position than anyone in the Aaronic priesthood to intercede between the people and God, so the Messiah took precedence in His priesthood above the temporal role of the high priest in the Temple.

Jesus the Messiah is a Mediator whom we can and will *see*. Through Him, we can see God, our heavenly Father, for He said: "Anyone who has *seen* me has seen the Father" (John 14:9), and "I and the Father are one" (10:30). When we gaze upon Jesus, we see the love of God. Jesus is the cleft of the rock where we can hide from the consuming fire of God's holiness. From our vantage point in Him, we can see the glory of God as well as His love without being devastated.

We need not fear the judgment of a holy God, for Jesus took upon Himself the wrath and judgment that rightfully are ours. We avoid God's devastating holiness by appropriating to ourselves the white robe of His righteousness to cover the nakedness of our sin. That robe of righteousness is the only covering (*kiporah*) in which we may appear before God and not be consumed, and He yearns to give us that covering that cost Him so much.

Jesus the Messiah paid a terrible price that we might belong to God in love. We humans find it incomprehensible that God, the Creator, would desire an intimate relationship with His creation. Nevertheless, He does seek a relationship with each member of the human race. He proposes a relationship that is even more personal than marriage.

God put the restoration of His relationship with humanity into motion through His people, Israel. He proposed to Abraham in Ur. He betrothed Himself to Israel at the Passover, and He married the nation at Mount Sinai. But Israel was no stronger in spiritual stamina than the rest of humanity around her. At times she has strayed and become an unfaithful wife to Jehovah. Despite this, He looks upon her with compassion and love and has promised to restore her once again, and with her, all other nations who are willing. Therefore, when the Messiah of Israel came as the Word made flesh, He proposed a loving relationship with God to all humanity. He betrothed Himself to those who would believe and accept Him at Calvary. The consummation of that marriage is yet to take place when He returns for His beloved, the bride called out from among believing Jews and Gentiles.

God is constantly inviting us. He told Abraham to leave Ur and follow Him. He invited the children of Israel to share the feast of the Passover Lamb, to leave Egypt and enter a new life. But God invites us all to do more than merely move from one location to another. He invites humanity to become something *for* Him. His invitation is an honor bestowed in love, but it is also the offer of an opportunity we dare not refuse.

God has prepared a feast of redemption and joy to which all are invited. The invitation is for us to come to the marriage supper of the Lamb, to come and partake of Jesus, the Bread of Life, the Lamb of God, the Mediator who has taken our judgment upon Himself.

Come to the marriage supper of the Lamb! He is the holy Bridegroom. He seeks as His bride all those who will give themselves to Him in love. He is the Holy Food that gives life and nourishment to the bride.

The Bible warns that everyone must deal with God's invitation. To those who will receive Him, Jesus is indeed the Lamb of God waiting to greet His beloved guests. But to those who spurn God's invitation of love, the Lamb will appear as the fierce Lion of the tribe of Judah (Revelation 5:5). To those who ignore God's invitation, He will be the roaring Lion whose authority has been challenged.

Come to the feast of redemption and joy! God invites you. With ardor He entreats you to accept the relationship of love. You are the guest to be honored by accepting His offer of abundant life in Christ.

Come to the feast of the Lamb! Come to the feast that God is preparing for those who love Him. All you need to gain entrance is your wedding garment, His robe of righteousness.

The Lamb who was once slain lives again. He has gone to prepare a place for those who trust Him. He has promised to come again and take His beloved to celebrate the festival of joy, to live eternally in perfect union with Him.

Will you accept the invitation that God offers? You can do this by a simple prayer. Acknowledge that you cannot face God in His holiness, and that you need His robe of righteousness. Confess that Jesus is the Messiah, the Lamb of God who takes away the sin of the world, that He died to make atonement for your sins and lives again to be your Mediator. Tell God that you desire to follow Him in the newness of His resurrection life.

Then find a body of believers who regularly commemorate the event of His death. By baptism be identified with Him in that death, and be identified with His people in the newness of life that He gives. Even as that Passover table of long ago brought the ancient Israelites from slavery to freedom, come now to the table that brings new life!

In the words of the psalmist, taste and see that the Lord is good. Then you will find within your heart a melody to sing a new song—the song of Moses and the song of the Lamb:

Great and marvelous are your deeds, Lord God Almighty. Just and true are your ways, King of the ages. Who will not fear you, O Lord, and bring glory to your name? For you alone are holy. All nations will come and worship before you, for your righteous acts have been revealed. (Revelation 15:3–4)

Come to God's feast! This is the song that one day will reverberate throughout the courts of heaven at that ultimate feast of freedom and joy.

The Spirit and the bride say, "Come!" And let him who hears say, "Come!" Whoever is thirsty, let him come; and whoever wishes, let him take the free gift of the water of life. (Revelation 22:17)

Appendix One—
Chart of Jewish Feasts

Feast	Season	Temporal Significance for Israel Under the Law	Future Significance for All God's People Under Grace	Scripture (KJV)	Event
PASSOVER	Spring (new beginning)	Redemption from bondage in Egypt	Believers in Christ redeemed from bondage of sin	"Ye were not redeemed with corruptible things, as silver and gold, . . . but with the precious blood of Christ, as of a lamb without blemish and without spot" (1 Peter 1:18–19).	THE CRUCIFIXION (Redemption)
UNLEAVENED BREAD	Spring (new life)	Purging of all leaven (symbol of sin)	All believers in Christ cleansed from sin and empowered to walk in newness of life	"Purge out . . . the old leaven, that ye may be a new lump . . . for even Christ our passover is sacrificed for us" (1 Corinthians 5:7).	(Santification)
				"[God] made him to be sin for us, who knew no sin; that we might be made the righteousness of God in him" (2 Corinthians 5:21).	(Justification)
FIRSTFRUITS	Spring (first of grain harvest)	Thanksgiving for firstfruits, the promise of the harvest to come (first of the grain presented to God)	Christ, the first to rise from the dead—the promise of resurrection and eternal life for all who believe in Him	"But now is Christ risen from the dead . . . the firstfruits of them that slept. . . . even so in Christ shall all be made alive" (1 Corinthians 15:20–22b).	THE RESURRECTION OF CHRIST
FEAST OF WEEKS (Pentecost)	Late spring seven weeks after Passover (ingathering of first harvest)	Thanksgiving for first harvest and	God's first harvest of those redeemed in Christ (Jews and Gentiles)	"And when the day of Pentecost was fully come, . . . they were all filled with the Holy Ghost. . . . the same day there were added unto them about three thousand souls" (Acts 2:1, 4, 41b).	THE COMING OF THE HOLY SPIRIT and
		(according to oral tradition) the time of the giving of the Law at Sinai	God's Law written on the hearts of the redeemed	"I will put my laws into their hearts, and in their minds will I write them" (Hebrews 10:16).	THE BIRTH OF THE CHURCH

(SUMMER, A TIME OF LABOR IN THE FIELDS AND PREPARATION FOR FINAL HARVEST. THE CHURCH AGE

Feast	Season	Temporal Significance for Israel Under the Law	Future Significance for All God's People Under Grace	Scripture (KJV)	Event
FEAST OF TRUMPETS	Early autumn	A solemn assembly (trumpets blown to prepare for the Day of Atonement)	The beginning of the regathering of Israel to the land in preparation for the final Day of Atonement	"I will gather them out of all countries, whither I have driven them . . . and I will bring them again unto this place, and I will cause them to dwell safely" (Jeremiah 32:37).	ISRAEL REGATHERED
			The assembly of all believers, dead and alive, in the heavens with Christ	"For the Lord himself shall descend from heaven with a shout, with the voice of the archangel, and with the trump of God: and the dead in Christ shall rise first: then we . . . shall be caught up together . . . to meet the Lord" (1 Thessalonians 4:16–17; see also 1 Corinthians 15:52)	THE RAPTURE OF THE CHURCH and THE RETURN OF CHRIST
DAY OF ATONEMENT	Autumn	A solemn assembly for repentance and forgiveness under the Law (repeated annually)	Believers in Christ forgiven by one atonement for all time	"So Christ was once offered to bear the sins of many" (Hebrews 9:28).	
			The rest of Israel of those redeemed in Christ (Jews and Gentiles)	"And I will pour upon the house of David, and upon the inhabitants of Jerusalem, the spirit of grace and of supplications: and they shall look upon me whom they have pierced, and they shall mourn for him. . . . In that day there shall be a fountain opened to the house of David and . . . Jerusalem for sin and for uncleanness" (Zechariah 12:10; 13:1).	ISRAEL TURNS TO HER MESSIAH
FEAST OF BOOTHS	Autumn (final harvest)	Harvest celebration and memorial of tabernacles in the wilderness	Joyous assembly— all peoples brought under the rule of the King Messiah	"Every one that is left of all the nations which came against Jerusalem shall even go up from year to year to worship the King, the LORD of hosts, and to keep the feast of tabernacles" (Zechariah 14:16).	THE KINGDOM OF GOD ON EARTH

Chart of Jewish Feasts

Sample Ceremony for the Celebration of Passover

T his Haggadah is adapted from traditional Jewish liturgy for use by Jewish or Gentile believers in Jesus who wish to conduct a Passover seder in either a congregational setting or a private home.

Passover Seder

1. The Lighting of the Candles

A woman from each table lights the candles. The leader explains:

LEADER: The Passover begins as the Woman of each household kindles the festival light and recites a traditional Jewish blessing. We have adapted the blessing to reflect our faith in Y'shua (Jesus) who is the light of the world.

LEADER: (Chants the blessing in Hebrew)

בָּרוּךְ אַתָּה, יְיָ אֱלֹהֵינוּ,
מֶלֶךְ הָעוֹלָם, אֲשֶׁר קִדְּשָׁנוּ
בְּיֵשׁוּעַ הַמָּשִׁיחַ, אוֹר הָעוֹלָם:

*Baruch atah, Adonai elohenu, melech ha-olam, asher kid'shanu
b'Y'shua ha-mashiach, or ha-olam.*

MOTHERS: Blessed are You, O Lord our God, King of the
universe, who has sanctified us in Jesus the Messiah, the
light of the world.

LEADER: It is most fitting that a woman kindles the lights,
for we are reminded of God's promise that the Messiah, the
light of the world, would come not from the seed of man, but
from the seed of woman and by the will of God. As the
prophet Isaiah declared:

MOTHERS: "A virgin shall conceive, and bear a son, and
shall call his name Immanuel" (Isaiah 7:14).

ALL: A light to lighten the Gentiles,

LEADER: and the glory of thy people Israel" (Luke 2:32).

ALL: Amen.

2. THE FIRST CUP: THE CUP OF SANCTIFICATION

LEADER: The Passover has begun and during the course of

our seder, we will drink from our cups and replenish them three more times.

All raise the first cup.

The first cup is called the Kiddush cup or the Cup of Sanctification.

ALL: With this cup, we commit our observance to the Lord, and pray for His blessing upon the rest of the service to follow.

LEADER: (Chants the blessing in Hebrew)

בָּרוּךְ אַתָּה, יְיָ אֱלֹהֵינוּ,
מֶלֶךְ הָעוֹלָם,
בּוֹרֵא פְּרִי הַגָּפֶן:

Baruch atah, Adonai elohenu, melech ha-olam, borei p'ree ha-gafen.

FATHERS: Blessed are You, O Lord our God, King of the universe, creator of the fruit of the vine.

ALL: Amen

LEADER: It was concerning this first cup that the Messiah declared:

ALL: "Take this, and divide it among yourselves: for I say unto you, I will not drink of the fruit of the vine, until the kingdom of God shall come" (Luke 22:17–18).

3. The Washing of Hands

LEADER: Ritual washings have been a part of Jewish life since God commanded Aaron to bathe his hands and feet before approaching the altar of the Lord. And so we customarily wash our hands at this time as a token of our desire to live lives of acceptable service to our Almighty God.

ALL: Yet Jesus carried this idea of servanthood one step further on that Passover night in the upper room. He "laid aside his garments, and took a towel, and girded Himself . . . and began to wash the disciples' feet" (John 13:4–5).

LEADER: How graciously has He taught us that the fullest meaning of servanthood is found in the attribute of humility.

ALL: "He that is greatest among you shall be your servant . . . and he that shall humble himself shall be exalted" (Matthew 23:11–12).

4. The Seder Plate

The leader points to the seder (pronounced "sey-der") plate and declares:

LEADER: Behold this seder plate and these traditional symbols that are placed on it.

ALL: What do they mean, and of what do they speak?

LEADER: The story of Passover is a story of our deliverance from bondage, and all of the elements of the Passover meal are part of the portrait of redemption. They are placed on this ceremonial plate for all at the table to see and partake of.

ALL: What is the meaning of the *karpas*, or greens, and the salt water?

LEADER: The greens remind us of life. The salt water represents tears. We immerse the greens in the salt water in thankfulness that we are redeemed, for we recognize that a life without redemption, is a life immersed in tears. The leader then chants the following blessing.

בָּרוּךְ אַתָּה, יְיָ אֱלֹהֵינוּ,
מֶלֶךְ הָעוֹלָם,
בּוֹרֵא פְּרִי הָאֲדָמָה:

Baruch atah, Adonai elohenu, melech ha'olam, borei p'ree ha'adamah.

ALL: Blessed are You, O Lord our God, King of the Universe, creator of the fruit of the earth.

All dip a piece of parsley in salt water and eat.

ALL: What is the meaning of the *chazereth* (hah-**zer**-it), the root of the bitter herb?

LEADER: The root reminds us of the bitterness of slavery in Egypt and the greater bitterness of slavery to sin. We are told as believers to "get rid of all bitterness, rage and anger, brawling and slander, along with every form of malice." And to "be kind and compassionate to one another, forgiving each other, just as in Christ God forgave you" (Ephesians 4:31–32).

ALL: And what is the meaning of the *maror* (mah-**roar**), the bitter herb itself?

LEADER: The bitter herb reminds us of the tears the Israelites shed when they were slaves in Egypt. We are to eat enough of the maror to allow our eyes to tear as well and also to remember that when Messiah returns "a fountain will be opened to the house of David and the inhabitants of Jerusalem, to cleanse them from sin and impurity" (Zechariah 13:1).

בָּרוּךְ אַתָּה, יְיָ אֱלֹהֵינוּ,
מֶלֶךְ הָעוֹלָם, אֲשֶׁר קִדְּשָׁנוּ
בְּמִצְוֹתָיו וְצִוָּנוּ עַל אֲכִלַת מָרוֹר:

*Baruch atah, Adonai elohenu, melech ha'olam, asher kid'shanu
b'mitzvohtav, vetzivahnu al achilat maror.*

ALL: Blessed are You, O Lord our God, King of the Universe, who has sanctified us by His commandments and commanded us to eat the bitter herb.

All eat a small helping of horseradish with matzo.

ALL: But what is the meaning of the *charoseth*, the apple mixture, and why is it sweet to the taste?

LEADER: The charoseth is reddish brown in color, like the color of the mortar with which the bricks were made by the Israelites for the storage cities of Egypt. We eat this to remind us of the hard labor of the Israelites.

CHRIST *in the Passover*

LEADER: (in Hebrew)

בָּרוּךְ אַתָּה, יְיָ אֱלֹהֵינוּ,
מֶלֶךְ הָעוֹלָם,
בּוֹרֵא פְּרִי הָאֲדָמָה:

Baruch atah, Adonai elohenu, melech ha'olam, borei p'ree ha-adamah.

ALL: Blessed are You, O Lord our God, King of the Universe, creator of the fruit of the earth.

The leader invites all to eat the charoseth. A small helping of charoseth with matzo is taken.

ALL: And what is the meaning of the egg, the *haggigah?* And why is it roasted?

LEADER: As a hen lays her eggs each morning, the roasted egg reminds us of the morning sacrifice at the Temple. However, the Temple no longer stands, and we mourn its destruction in AD 70 by dipping the haggigah into salt water, which represents tears. The haggigah is also cause for rejoicing, that Jesus, the perfect, once and for all sacrifice can bring us peace and fellowship with God. The Scripture says of Him, "But now he has appeared once for all at the end of the ages to do away with sin by the sacrifice of himself" (Hebrews 9:26).

The Leader invites all to eat the haggigah dipped in salt water.

ALL: And what is the meaning of the *zeroah*, the shank bone of the lamb?

LEADER: The zeroah reminds us of the Passover lamb that was sacrificed in Egypt, its blood put on the doorposts of the Israelite homes as a sign, so that death would pass over those homes. The zeroah reminds us of the Lamb of God who was sacrificed for us.

5. THE BREAD OF AFFLICTION

LEADER: Rabbi Gamaliel said, "He who has not explained the three symbols of the seder has not fulfilled his duty: the Passover lamb, the bitter herb, and the unleavened bread."

ALL: We have heard of the Paschal lamb and we have eaten of the bitter herb, but what of the unleavened bread?

The leader holds up a piece of matzo.

LEADER: Behold the bread of affliction which the Israelites (our ancestors) ate in the land of Egypt. Then they (we) were slaves, now they (we) are free. Let all who are hungry come and eat.

ALL: But what is the meaning of this unleavened bread?

LEADER: The unleavened bread reminds us that our redemption out of Egypt came quickly as the Israelites left in haste without time for the dough of their bread to rise and become leavened. For during Passover, no leavened foods can be eaten. No items that have touched leaven can remain in the home. A ceremony to remove the leaven takes place the night before Passover begins. Leaven is also symbolic of sin. Perhaps this sheds additional light on the words of Paul, who wrote, "Purge out therefore the old leaven, that ye may be a new lump, as ye are unleavened. For even Christ our passover is sacrificed for us. Therefore let us keep the feast, not with old leaven, neither with the leaven of malice and wickedness, but with the unleavened bread of sincerity and truth" (1 Corinthians 5:7–8).

6. THE MATZO TASH

The leader lifts the matzo tash and refers to the stack of three matzos on each table.

LEADER: This three-compartment pouch contains three pieces of matzo, yet it is also called a unity. There are several explanations for this three in one unity. Some say it is a unity of worship: of the priests, the Levites, and the entire congregation of Israel. Some say it is a unity of the patriarchs: Abraham, Isaac, and Jacob. However the center wafer is removed, broken, and wrapped in linen to be brought back at a later time. As believers we see a greater unity represented here—the unity of God: God the Father, God the Son, and God the Holy Spirit.

This centerpiece of matzo, now broken, has a special name: the *afikomen*. This is not a Hebrew word, but a Greek word, and it means, "That which comes after." The origin and significance of the afikomen and the matzo tash are shadowed in mystery—a mystery we will explore as our celebration unfolds. But for now, guesses must give way to a game.

The leader explains the game.

LEADER: We are going to hide the afikomen as you children close your eyes. If you find it, we have to buy it back from you, or the Passover cannot be concluded. And remember . . .

ALL: Great is the reward of the one who finds the hidden afikomen.

7. THE FOUR QUESTIONS

LEADER: The children are essential to the Passover celebration, for it is through this feast that they may learn of God's redemptive nature. And so at this time, the children come forward to learn the meaning of Passover by asking the traditional four questions. Who will ask the four questions for all the children?

CHILD: Why is this night different from all other nights?

FATHERS: Once the Israelites were slaves to Pharaoh in Egypt, but the Lord in His goodness and mercy redeemed them (us) from that land with a mighty hand and an outstretched arm.

ALL: Had He not redeemed them (us), surely they (we) and their (our) children would still be enslaved.

CHILD: On all other nights we eat either leavened or unleavened bread; on this night why do we eat only unleavened bread?

FATHERS: We eat the unleavened bread to remember that the sons of Israel, in their haste to leave Egypt, had to take their bread with them while it was still flat.

CHILD: On all other nights, we eat herbs of every kind; on this night, why do we eat only bitter herbs?

FATHERS: We eat the bitter herbs to remember how bitter it is to be enslaved.

CHILD: On all other nights we do not dip the sop even once; on this night, why do we dip twice?

FATHERS: By dipping, we remember that a life of bondage is bitter indeed, but that even the harshest bondage is sweetened by the promise of redemption.

CHILD: On all other nights, we eat our meal in any manner; why is this night so special?

FATHERS: This night is truly special; for once the Israelites (we) were slaves, but now they (we) are free, so we recline in order to appropriate and appreciate the rest God has wrought for us.

LEADER: By strength of hand, the Lord brought Israel (us) out of Egypt, from the house of bondage. In gratitude, let us then worship our God and recount the story of Passover.

8. THE STORY OF PASSOVER

ALL: And just as the blood of those first Passover lambs was applied in faith to the doorposts of Israel's homes, so the blood of the Messiah must be applied in faith to the door-posts of our hearts. And so tonight, we worship God not only because the angel of death passed over the Jewish people's homes,

LEADER: But because all of us—whether Jewish or Gentile—may be redeemed from an even greater bondage, the bondage of sin, through faith in the Messiah of Israel.

ALL: The Messiah Jesus.

LEADER: Through Him, we may pass over from death to life.

ALL: Amen.

9. THE TEN PLAGUES

LEADER: A full cup is a symbol of complete joy. Let us, therefore, diminish our cups as we recall the plagues that befell the Egyptians.

The leader recites the plagues one at a time and all respond (e.g., Leader: Blood, All: Blood) as participants use one finger to empty a drop from the cup onto a plate or saucer for each plague.

The plagues: Blood—Frogs—Lice—Flies—Cattle Disease—Boils—Hail—Locusts—Darkness—Slaying of the Firstborn.

10. THE SECOND CUP: THE CUP OF PRAISE

LEADER: It is now time to drink the second cup.

All raise their cups.

LEADER: (in Hebrew)

בָּרוּךְ אַתָּה, יְיָ אֱלֹהֵינוּ,
מֶלֶךְ הָעוֹלָם,
בּוֹרֵא פְּרִי הַגָּפֶן:

Baruch atah, Adonai elohenu, melech ha'olam, borei p'ree ha-gafen.

ALL: Blessed are You, O Lord our God, creator of the fruit of the vine. We praise you, not for the plagues that brought suffering, but for Israel's deliverance that followed.

All drink the second cup.

Sing a song with deliverance theme.

11. THE LEADER'S GRACE BEFORE DINNER

12. THE PASSOVER MEAL

Dinner is served.

13. THE AFIKOMEN

The leader now sends the children in search of the hidden afikomen. The child who finds the afikomen returns it to the leader and receives a reward.

The leader raises the matzo.

LEADER: This joy over the afikomen is certainly one of the more delightful moments of the Passover seder. And you see, some mystery surrounds the significance of the afikomen and the matzo tosh from which it has been drawn. We may justly ask,

ALL: What is the meaning of the three matzos, and why is the middle matzo broken, buried, and then brought back?

LEADER: To many people the question is a riddle to be resolved. But for those who know the Messiah, it need not be a riddle at all. For where can we find a clearer picture of our Messiah than in this tradition concerning the afikomen that has been broken . . . buried . . . and then brought back? Even the matzo, a symbol of a sinless nature, speaks of Jesus. The rabbis have set down some very specific regulations concerning the appearance of matzo. If it is to be found suitable for Passover use, first it must be striped . . .

ALL: As was Jesus. For the prophet Isaiah says, "And with his stripes we are healed" (Isaiah 53:5).

LEADER: Second, it must be pierced.

ALL: As was Jesus. For the prophet Zechariah says: "They shall look upon me whom they have pierced" (Zechariah 12:10).

LEADER: Earlier we called this the bread of affliction that the Israelites (our ancestors) ate in the land of Egypt. And this is true. But it is also a symbol of the Bread of Life, which comes down from heaven, and gives life to the world. Jesus said:

ALL: "I am the bread of life: he that cometh to me shall never hunger; and he that believeth on me shall never thirst" (John 6:35).

LEADER: Let all who are hungry come and eat.

The matzo is eaten.

14. THE THIRD CUP: THE CUP OF REDEMPTION

The third cup is filled.

ALL: What is the meaning of the third cup, the cup of redemption, the cup taken after the dinner meal?

LEADER: The promise of God to redeem the enslaved Israelites with an outstretched arm is available to us as well. Jesus took this third cup, the cup after the meal, and said, "For this is my blood of the new testament, which is shed for many for the remission of sins" (Matthew 26:28).

All drink the third cup.

15. COMMUNION: THE LORD'S SUPPER

16. THE FOURTH CUP: THE CUP OF HALLEL

The fourth cup is filled.

LEADER: Now comes the recitation from the Hallel or Praise Psalms, 113 through 118. Let us recite psalms of worship at this time, just as Jesus recited them every year as part of His Passover observance. Praise you the Lord!

ALL: Praise, O you servants of the Lord, praise the name of the Lord.

LEADER: Blessed be the name of the Lord from this time forth and forevermore.

ALL: From the rising of the sun to the going down of the same, the Lord's name is to be praised.

LEADER: The Lord is high above all nations, and His glory above the heavens.

ALL: Who is like unto the Lord, our God, who dwells on high?

LEADER: Give thanks to the Lord, for He is good.

ALL: For His love endures forever!

LEADER: I love the Lord, for He heard my voice; He heard my cry for mercy.

ALL: Because He turned His ear to me, I will call on Him as long as I live.

LEADER: The Lord is gracious and righteous; our God is full of compassion.

ALL: The Lord protects the simple-hearted; when I was in great need, He saved me.

LEADER: How can I repay the Lord for all His goodness to me?

ALL: I will lift up the cup of salvation and call on the name of the Lord.

LEADER: Praise the Lord, all you nations; extol Him, all you peoples.

ALL: For great is His love toward us, and the faithfulness of the Lord endures forever. Praise the Lord.

LEADER: Shouts of joy and victory resound in the tents of the righteous.

ALL: The Lord's right hand has done mighty things!

LEADER: I will not die but live and proclaim what the Lord has done.

ALL: The Lord has chastened me severely but He has not given me over to death.

LEADER: The stone the builders rejected has become the capstone.

ALL: The Lord has done this, and it is marvelous in our eyes.

LEADER: You are my God and I will give thanks. You are my God, and I will exalt You.

ALL: Give thanks to the Lord, for He is good; His love endures forever.

All drink the fourth cup.

17. THE CUP OF ELIJAH (not taken)

The leader points to the cup of Elijah.

LEADER: The sharing of the afikomen and the cup of redemption are precious moments in the Passover seder. Yet many of God's beloved chosen people do not yet see how the Messiah and His promise to redeem them are portrayed in the breaking of this bread and the drinking of this cup. And so they look ahead to the promise represented by a special cup set aside for the prophet Elijah. It is recorded by the Hebrew prophet Malachi that the Messiah's coming will be preceded by the return of Elijah the prophet. And each year at Passover, a child goes to the door and opens it wide, hoping the prophet will accept the invitation, enter the home, and announce the coming of the Messiah.

A cherished Jewish prayer is for the prophet Elijah to come soon, in our time, with the Messiah, Son of David. Yet, we know that Elijah has returned. For when Jesus spoke of the prophet John, He said of him, "If ye will receive it, this is Elias, which was for to come" (Matthew 11:14). The prophet, the forerunner, has come. And so did the Messiah, even during Passover some two thousand years ago.

18. INVITATION

19. THE HOPE

LEADER: As we celebrate this Passover seder, may our hearts be joined in gratitude to God for the coming of Messiah, for His death and resurrection, and for the promise of His return.

ALL: Praise the Lord, all you nations; praise Him all you people. For His merciful kindness is great toward us, and the truth of the Lord endures forever. Hallelujah!

LEADER: It is traditional to conclude the seder with the words, "L'Shana Ha Ba'ah B'yerushalayim" which means "Next Year in Jerusalem." For generations, this greeting has captured the fervent hope of the Jewish people, a hope to be restored to the ancient land of Israel, to Jerusalem, in the presence of the Messiah Himself.

We too have a similar precious hope, the hope of Messiah's soon return.

We believe in the surety of His promise: "Behold, I am coming soon! My reward is with me, and I will give to everyone according to what he has done. I am the Alpha and the Omega, the First and the Last, the Beginning and the End. . . . I am the Root and the Offspring of David, and the bright Morning Star." (Revelation 22:12, 16)

LEADER and ALL: Maranatha! Come, Lord Jesus!

COMPARING ASHKENAZIC AND SEPHARDIC PASSOVER CUSTOMS OF NORTH AMERICA

S*ephardim* are Jews from Mediterranean and Spanish countries. *Ashkenazim* are Jews of Eastern European descent. Out of a total Jewish population of slightly more than six million in North America, less than two hundred thousand are Sephardim. Sephardic Passover customs often differ from those of the Ashkenazim. Occasionally there is partial overlap with the Ashkenazic customs, but the distinctive foods and languages of the Sephardic tradition add their own special flavor.

In this chart Judeo-Spanish = from the Balkans and the Levant (eastern Mediterranean countries); Spanish and Portuguese = from Amsterdam, Holland.

Ashkenazic Customs and Practices	Sephardic Customs and Practices	Sephardic Community
Bedikat chometz (searching out and cleansing leaven from the home) The housewife places a few crumbs of leaven (bread, crackers, etc.) in a conspicuous spot. The husband finds it in a ceremonial search, using a candle, a feather, and a wooden spoon. He wraps it in a napkin and takes it to be burned at the local synagogue site or another designated area.	The housewives wrap ten pieces of bread in plastic or another material. The men search for the pieces and set them aside to be burned the next day in the street.	Syrian
	The wives hide ten pieces of bread with slices of grilled liver. As in Syria, the men find the pieces so they can be burned.	Moroccan
	The wives make up a plate with ten pieces of bread. The men search for it with a candle, sweeping up the bread with the remains of the *lulav* (the "rod" of branches used during the holiday of Succoth). The bread is burned the next day.	Judeo-Spanish
	A small amount of bread is hidden, not necessarily ten pieces. The men search for it with a candle and a feather.	Spanish and Portuguese

Ashkenazic Customs and Practices	Sephardic Customs and Practices	Sephardic Community
Ta'anit bechorot (Feast of the Firstborn) Commemoration of the saving of the firstborn Israelites on the first Passover eve, it is found among the Ashkenazim, but is not a widespread practice.	On the day before Passover, every firstborn son and daughter fasts and attends the morning service. This service marks the conclusion of learning a tractate of the Talmud and is followed by a *se'udah*, or festival meal, ending the fast (observed particularly among the Syrian Jews).	Syrian Spanish and Portuguese
Seder Plate A ceremonial platter with divided areas for holding the symbolic foods of the Passover seder, especially those commanded in Exodus 12:8. Ashkenazic Jews generally follow the arrangement of Rabbi Isaac Luria, as explained in the next column.	Called the *keara*, this centerpiece of the Passover seder is set according to the tradition of Rabbi Isaac Luria. Each of the foods originally represented one of the *Ten Sefirot* (Jewish mystical representations), though few Jews today subscribe to the tenets of Jewish mysticism. The items are set out in the form of a Star of David.	Syrian Moroccan Judeo-Spanish
	The items are set out on three separate plates.	Spanish and Portuguese

Ashkenazic Customs and Practices	Sephardic Customs and Practices	Sephardic Community
Charoseth Ashkenazic Jews use a mixture of apples, nuts, cinnamon, and wine to symbolize the brickmaking of the enslaved Israelites.	A mixture of crushed dates, almonds, and wine	Syrian
	A mixture of apples, nuts, figs, dates, black raisins, and wine	Judeo-Spanish
	A mixture of almonds, apples, raisins, spices, and wine (in Surinam they also use coconut.)	Spanish and Portuguese
Cup of Elijah Wine is taken in anticipation of Elijah's return to herald the coming of the Messiah.	Though it is normally an Ashkenazic practice, Syrian Jews have adopted the inclusion of the cup in the seder.	Syrian
The Elements of the Seder: *Yachatz* (breaking the middle piece of a triple stack of wafers of unleavened bread)	The matzo (unleavened bread) is broken into the shape of the Hebrew letters *dalet* and *vav*. Hebrew letters are also used as numbers: *dalet* (4) + *vav* (6) = 10, showing that the matzo symbolically represents the *Ten Sefirot*.	Syrian

Ashkenazic Customs and Practices	Sephardic Customs and Practices	Sephardic Community
	The matzo is broken into the shape of the Hebrew letter *heh*. Then each seder participant holds a piece against his or her eyes and recites, "This is the bread of affliction."	Moroccan
The Afikomen Half of the middle piece of matzo is wrapped in a special cloth or bag and hidden early in the seder. In Ashkenazic practice the children find it and hold it for ransom, to be redeemed by the head of the feast so it may be divided and eaten after the meal.	It is wrapped in a special cloth, then thrown over the shoulder as participants recite, "Their kneading troughs being bound up in their clothes upon their shoulders. And the children of Israel did according to the word of Moses" (taken from Exodus 12:34–35 KJV). Then in Arabic the following is recited: "Where do you come from?" "Egypt!" "Where are you going?" "To Jerusalem!"	Syrian
	The leader leaves the room and returns with a staff and the wrapped afikomen over his shoulder. A dramatic recitation of the Exodus follows.	Moroccan

Ashkenazic Customs and Practices	Sephardic Customs and Practices	Sephardic Community
	The leader leaves the room, then returns with a staff, a tightened belt, and a sack containing the afikomen over his shoulder. The same questions are asked as among the Syrians. Then each participant carries the afikomen on his or her shoulder as though traveling from Egypt to Israel.	Judeo-Spanish
The Four Questions Beginning with "Why is this night different from all other nights?" the questions describe the seder rituals and ask what they mean.	The questions are the same, but the order differs among the Sephardim. Ashkenazim ask about eating matzo, eating bitter herbs, dipping twice, and reclining. Sephardim ask about dipping twice, eating matzo, eating bitter herbs, and reclining.	All Sephardic Groups

Ashkenazic Customs and Practices	Sephardic Customs and Practices	Sephardic Community
The Ten Plagues Usually ten drops of wine are poured or dipped out into a saucer with a finger-tip, one for each plague, to commemorate God's ten acts of judgment on Egypt. (Occasionally Ashkenazic practice is similar to the Sephardic practice.)	Sixteen drops of wine are poured: three for "blood," "fire," and "pillars of smoke"; ten for the ten plagues, and three more for words whose letters form an acronym for the names of the plagues.	Syrian
	Thirteen drops are used; ten for the plagues and three for the acronym. The drops are poured into a basin, and no one may look at them.	Judeo-Spanish
	Thirteen drops are poured out.	Spanish and Portuguese
The Seder Meal Ashkenazim eat foods originating from Eastern Europe rather than from Mediterranean or Spanish countries.	The seder meal includes rice and *kibe*, which for Passover is meat wrapped in a matzo-meal shell.	Syrian
Eating the Afikomen It is the last food eaten; nothing is said about it.	As they partake of it, participants recite, "in memory of the Passover lamb, the afikomen is eaten."	Syrian

OTHER PASSOVER CUSTOMS DISTINCTIVE
TO VARIOUS SEPHARDIC GROUPS

Syrian Jews visit the rabbi and his family at home, and in a *leil chometz* ceremony on the last night of Passover, the men beat each other with stalks of wheat to symbolize hope for a fruitful year.

During Passover week, **Moroccan** Jews have a special children's seder and a ceremony of blessing the newly blossoming trees. After the end of Passover they have the *Maimuna* festival, a joyous time for picnics, parties initiating courtships, and exchanging good wishes for a successful year. Moroccan Jews do not eat black olives during Passover month (Nisan) because they are said to cause forgetfulness, and Jews must be careful to remember the story of redemption at Passover.

In a **Judeo-Spanish** custom the grandfather or father picks fresh grass on the last night of Passover and brings it home. He throws it on the floor along with money and candy, and the children pick it up, symbolizing hope for a good summer and a successful year.

Based on information in Herbert C. Dobrinsky, A *Treasury of Sephardic Laws and Customs: The Ritual Practices of Syrian, Moroccan, Judeo-Spanish and Spanish and Portuguese Jews of North America,* revised edition (Hoboken, N.J.: Ktav Publishing House, Inc. and New York: Yeshiva University Press, 1988).

A Chronological Look at the Passion Week

Saturday and Sunday

Jesus drew near to Jerusalem,[1] arriving at Bethany six days before Passover,[2] which was the Saturday before the Passion. Jesus was anointed at Simon the leper's house.[3] On Sunday, there was a great crowd that came to Bethany to see Jesus.[4]

Monday

The next day[5] was Jesus' triumphal entry into Jerusalem,[6] followed by His visit to the temple,[7] and His return to Bethany. It was Nisan 10, when the Passover lambs were selected. Likewise, the triumphal entry was the day when Christ presented Himself as Israel's Paschal Lamb.

Tuesday

On the way from Bethany to Jerusalem, Jesus cursed the fig tree,[8] and He cleansed the temple in Jerusalem.[9] Some religious leaders began to plot ways to kill Him. That evening Jesus left Jerusalem, presumably returning to Bethany.[10]

WEDNESDAY

On the way to Jerusalem, the disciples saw the withered fig tree.[11] At the temple in Jerusalem, Jesus' authority and wisdom was questioned by some religious leaders.[12] That afternoon Jesus went to the Mount of Olives and delivered the Olivet Discourse.[13] Two additional things occurred on that day: (1) Jesus predicted that in two days He would be crucified at the time of the Passover;[14] and (2) Judas planned the betrayal of Christ with some religious leaders.[15]

THURSDAY

Jesus and His disciples prepared the Passover lamb,[16] and they had their Passover meal in the Upper Room.[17] Jesus shared powerful truth with His disciples and offered an intercessory prayer in their behalf.[18] They arrived at the Garden of Gethsemane, where Jesus suffered in agony awaiting what was to come.[19] Later that night Jesus was betrayed and arrested.[20] He was tried first by Annas and later by Caiaphas and other religious leaders.[21]

FRIDAY

Early in the morning, Jesus was tried by the Sanhedrin, Pilate, Herod Antipas, and Pilate again.[22] He was led to the cross and crucified at 9:00 a.m. and died at 3:00 p.m. and was buried later that day.[23] Christ the Paschal Lamb (1 Corinthians 5:7) died at the time when the Israelites were sacrificing their Passover lambs.

CHRIST in the Passover

SATURDAY

Jesus' body was in the tomb during the Sabbath, and the Pharisees hired Roman guards to keep watch of the tomb.[24]

SUNDAY

Christ was resurrected from the dead.[25] His was the first of many resurrections to come, in which it was a type of first fruits offering. (First fruits offerings were made by Jews on the day after the Sabbath.)[26]

Verse References:
1. JOHN 11:55
2. JOHN 12:1
3. MATT. 26:6–13; MARK 14:3–9; JOHN 12:1–8
4. JOHN 12:9–11
5. JOHN 12:12
6. MATT. 21:1–9; MARK 11:1–10; LUKE 19:28–40; JOHN 12:12–19
7. MATT. 21:10–11; MARK 11:11
8. MATT. 21:18–19; MARK 11:12–14
9. MATT. 21:12–13; MARK 11:15–17; LUKE 19:45–46
10. MARK 11:18–19; LUKE 19:47–48
11. MATT. 21:20–22; MARK 11:20–26
12. MATT. 21:23–23:39; MARK 11:27–12:44; LUKE 20:1–21:4
13. MATT. 24:1–25:46; MARK 13:1–27; LUKE 21:5–36
14. MATT. 26:1–5; MARK 141–2; LUKE 22:1–2
15. MATT. 26:14–16; MARK 14:10–11; LUKE 22:3–6
16. MATT. 26:17–19; MARK 14:12–16; LUKE 22:7–13
17. MATT. 26:20–30; MARK 14:17–26; LUKE 22: 14–30
18. MATT. 26:30–35; MARK 14:26–31; LUKE 22:31–39; JOHN 15:1–18:1)
19. MATT. 26:36–46; MARK 14:32–42; LUKE 22: 39–46; JOHN 18:1
20. MATT. 26:46–56; MARK 14:43–52; LUKE 22:47–53; JOHN 18:2–12
21. MATT. 26:57–75; MARK 14:53–72; LUKE 22:54–65; JOHN 18: 13–27
22. MATT. 27:1–30; MARK 15:1–19; LUKE 22:66–23:25; JOHN 18:28–19:16
23. MATT. 27:31–60; MARK 15:20–46; LUKE 23:26–54; JOHN 19:16–42
24. MATT. 27:61–66; MARK 15:47; LUKE 23:55–56
25. MATT. 28:1–15; MARK 16:1–9[9–13]; LUKE 24:1–35
26. LEV. 23:9–14; 1 COR. 15:23

Adapted from *Chronological Aspects of the Life of Christ* by Harold W. Hoehner. Copyright c. 1977 by The Zondervan Corporation 1973, 1974 by Dallas Theological Seminary. Used by permission of the The Zondervan Corporation.

THE RECKONING OF PASSOVER

THURSDAY	Galilean Method Synoptic Reckoning Used by Jesus, His Disciples, and Pharisees	Judean Method John's Reckoning Used by Sadducees	Midnight
	Nisan 14 3-5 p.m. Passover Lamb Slain		Sunrise
Last Supper Jesus Arrested		Nisan 14	Sunset
FRIDAY			Midnight
6 a.m. Jesus before Pilate 9 a.m. Crucifixion 12–3 p.m. Darkness 3 p.m. Jesus Died Jesus Buried	Nisan 15	3-5 p.m. Passover Lamb Slain	Sunrise
		Nisan 15	Sunset
SATURDAY	⇓	⇓	Midnight

© 1974 by Dallas Theological Seminary. This chart may not be reproduced in any form without prior written permission.

NOTES

1. By tradition, the Jewish celebrate fiscal New Year in the fall, in the seventh month of the Jewish calendar, but the religious calendar begins in Nisan, the first month.

2. Arthur W. Pink, *Gleanings in Exodus* (Chicago: Moody, n.d.), 93.

3. A word study on the "arm of the Lord" is particularly interesting in connection with the rescue from Egypt.

4. Pink, 89–90.

5. Once, in Matthew 13:33, it is used as a symbol of growth and expansion.

6. Pink, 93.

7. Each Jewish person, for all time, must consider himself or herself, personally, as one whom the Lord delivered from bondage.

8. See Acts 2:9–11.

9. Even in modern times the Hebrew word used for visiting Jerusalem is *aliyah*, which means "going up."

10. Such a stable in Bethlehem sheltered Mary and Joseph at the birth of Jesus.

11. Alfred Edersheim, *The Temple, Its Ministry and Services as They Were at the Time of Jesus Christ* (Grand Rapids: Eerdmans, 1954), 220.

12. This is why Jesus cried out in anger: "It is written . . . 'My house will be called a house of prayer,' but you are making it a 'den of robbers'" (Matthew 21:13, cf. Mark 11:15–17; Luke 19:45–46).

13. Some sources indicate there were two flat cakes of unleavened bread; others say there were three.

14. The command to expound on the story of redemption is mentioned three times: Exodus 10:2; 12:26–27; and 13:8.

15. Epiphanius, *Panarion Haer*, 70.10; Eusebius, *Eccles. Hist*, 5.23.

16. Solomon Zeitlin, *The Jewish Quarterly Review* 28, no. 4 (April 1948).

17. "Not one stone here will be left on another; every one will be thrown down" (Matthew 24:2; Mark 13:2; Luke 21:6).

18. Matthew 26:17; Mark 14:12; Luke 22:1. Josephus once called it "a feast for eight days" (*Antiquites* 2.15:1; cf. 3.10.5 and 9.13.3).

19. This prayer is called the *Kal Hamira*. Cf. chap. 5, 57.

20. If horseradish is difficult to obtain, some people use a whole onion or a whole, large, white radish.

21. Chapter 3, 36.

22. Herbert Bronstein, ed., *The New Union Haggadag*, rev. ed., 15.

23. Cf. chap. 6, 64–66.

24. See "Kitel," *Encyclopedia Judaica* (Jerusalem: Keter, 1971), 10: 364.

25. Jewish men wear small head coverings (yarmulke) when they pray. The miter described in the text is usually reserved for the cantor who leads the synagogue worship. At Passover the host, as religious leader of the evening, may wear the miter.

26. By rabbinic tradition, an olive-sized morsel is the smallest over which a person can say a blessing.

27. Herbert Bronstein, ed., *The New Union Haggadah* (New York: Central Conference of American Rabbis, 1975, rev. ed.), 91.

28. Jewish people already living in Israel say instead: "Next year in Jerusalem rebuilt!"

29. Cf. chapter 7, 81.

30. Chaim Raphael, *A Feast of History* (New York: Simon & Schulsinger, 1958), 86.

31. Ibid., 95 (italics added).

32. Due to geographic factors, Sephardic culture and tradition (and even the pronunciation of the Hebrew language itself) bear the closest link to that Judaism that was practiced in the Holy Land before the final dispersion.

INDEX

Note: Page numbers in italics indicate illustrations

A FINAL NOTE

For information about live and media
presentations of the Passover seder, please
contact us at Jews for Jesus. Additional
resources and testimonies of Jewish
believers in Jesus are available at
www.jewsforjesus.org

Jews for Jesus
60 Haight Street
San Francisco, California 94102
e-mail: jfj@jewsforjesus.org

For Passover specific recipes,
charts, and more:
recipes.jewsforjesus.org
resources.jewsforjesus.org

More from Moody Publishers . . .

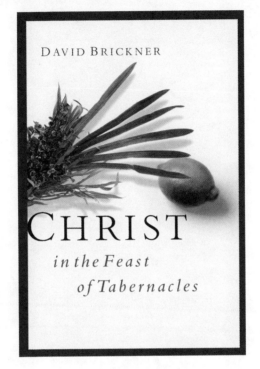

ISBN: 0-8024-1396-X

Why was it at the Feast of Tabernacles that Jesus said, "I am the Light of the World" and "Come to me and drink"? In the early days this festival was celebrated by erecting temporary shelters to demonstrate the transience of life; over the years meaningful new practices were added. You'll find *Christ in the Feast of Tabernacles* an intriguing read as you learn how the elements of this joyful and prophetic festival come together while Jesus both tabernacles with us now and is preparing an everlasting tabernacle for those who love Him.